technical trading online

Wiley Online Trading for a Living

technical trading online

TRADER X

AS TOLD TO

JEROLD ROTH

JOHN WILEY & SONS, INC.

New York • Chichester • Weinheim • Brisbane • Singapore • Toronto

Library of Congress Cataloging-in-Publication Data:

ISBN 0-471-39421-1

Printed in the United States of America.

10 9 8 7 6 5 4 3 2 1

preface

Recently, on one of the network all night news programs, a British correspondent gave an example of how the insanity of dot.com stock prices in the United States had supposedly driven the British securities market nuts. His example was an old-line, medium-size, consistently profitable corporation. This corporation happened to own a large block of stock in a yet-to-be-profitable, wet-behind-the-ears, dot.com high flyer. The value of this block of stock exceeded the value of all outstanding stock of the old-line company.

Think about that. Part ownership of an unprofitable company is worth more than entire ownership of a profitable one. Okay, that's possible. It has to be, at least according to something called Faure's Law, which states: "If it happens, it must be possible." Yet is it logical?

A closer examination of this case will push logic to its extremes, if not over the edge. What would happen if the old-line company split itself into two companies, the second one consisting of nothing more than the dot.com stock. Logically, the old-line company would drop in value, and the dot.com holding company would assume the market value of its sole asset, the block of dot.com stock. Yet, this would not and could not happen. The old-line company, by divesting itself of this valuable asset, would actually increase in value.

Hard to believe? Then look again. The value of the block of dot.com stock is worth more than all outstanding shares of the company that owns it. This means that if you take away this dot.com stock, the company that owns it should have a negative value. In other words, stock traders have valued the stock of an as-yet-to-be-profitable dot.com company at countless times its weight in gold. On the other hand, they have given the old-line, medium-size, consistently profitable corporation, subtracting the dot.com stock, a minus value. This value would cross over to positive if the old-line company took all its valuable dot.com stock certificates and burned them for heat. Logical? If you are looking for logic, don't look at today's stock market.

If you are looking for discussions of price/earnings ratios, do not waste your time looking within this book. You will not find any, nor will you find the wisdom to explain today's stock market. You certainly will not find a secret method for guaranteed profits. What you will find in *Technical Trading Online* is a substantial amount of hard-earned knowledge, knowledge I paid for with many long years and many costly mistakes. I am sure that I'm not the first person to tell you that knowledge is money, but I may be the first to add that this is especially true in the stock market.

If you have as yet to decide if this book is really for you, perhaps I can save you the bother of reading it. *Technical Trading Online* is not written for people looking to amuse themselves by trading stocks. If you are searching for amusement, allow me to suggest Las Vegas. Not only is Las Vegas far more amusing than the stock markets, you can probably amuse yourself far longer before eventually going broke. Nor is this book written for people interested in trading stocks because it seems the trendy thing to do. Believe me, by the time you perfect your trading skills, something else, surely less demanding, will be the trendy thing to do. One last type of person I would dissuade from buying this book is the kind looking for "juice."

preface

If you are literally looking for juice, save a hell of a bundle by buying a Juicerator©. If you are looking for the type of "juice" sometimes referred to as a rush, allow me to steer you instead toward bungee jumping or sky diving. Either of these activities will cost you less money in the long run. And if you don't happen to survive the short run, cleaning up your mistakes will be someone else's problem. However, if you insist on both "juice" and profit, robbing banks is probably just the thing for you. At the very least, it will offer you more favorable odds than trading stocks.

Then who is this book written for? *Technical Trading Online* is written for those people who come to trading for one single, overriding purpose—to make money.

This book will add to your knowledge by providing strategies, techniques, and plain tricks that could and should prove very valuable when applied to today's stock markets. Equally important, it will tell you how to take advantage of various stores of knowledge and countless sources of data now available online. No book can tell you all you need to know, but rest assured, by reading *Technical Trading Online,* you will gain substantial knowledge not provided by any currently available book. I am confident you will come to value the following material far, far more than the price paid for it or the time spent reading it.

TRADER X

September 2000

contents

contents

chapter 1

the golden rules
of stock trading

sinners, abandon all hope here

Tempting as it is to be cleverly innovative, let's start this book at the basic, solid, ground floor beginning. If you are determined *not* to learn anything valuable from *Technical Trading Online,* even by accident, the most important things *not* to learn are the Four Golden Rules of Stock Trading. Fair warning now: If you do learn them, and subsequently fail to follow them, they will come back to haunt you after every disastrous trading day. There you will be, trying to blame your losses on bad luck, bad advice, bad information, bad fate, bad food, bad coffee, bad influences, bad digestion, bad karma, bad weather, bad genes, bad service, bad air, bad circulation, bad company, perhaps even bad breath. Yet deep down you will know that the critical condition of your still-bleeding balance sheet is the result of disobeying one or more of the Four Golden Rules of Stock Trading. You will refuse to admit this at first, even to yourself. Yet, deep down, you will know.

Learning how to trade stocks effectively takes more than books, advice, and practice. It takes time—the more the better. Much of this time will be spent losing money. Yet I strongly believe that if you follow the Four Golden Rules of Stock Trading, you should be able to stretch your capital far enough to start turning some profits.

The Four Golden Rules of Stock Trading are:

1. Cut your losses.
2. Let your profits run.
3. Trade with the trend.
4. Never average down your losing positions.

There is not one of these rules you should find surprising or suspect. In fact, you are probably thinking that they are pretty much commonsense rules that you would follow naturally. You may be right, but I doubt it. Next time you have a bad day at the market, think about these rules again. I can just about guarantee that you broke at least one of them.

rule 1   cut your losses

Trading stocks is a profession that encompasses the making of mistakes, if not by definition, at least by the law of averages. I've never met a trader who didn't make mistakes. Please forgive my skepticism that you will be the first.

You will make mistakes because trading is not a science. It is an art—an art that is based on judgment, and this judgment is based on knowledge, and this knowledge can never be perfect. Fortunately, it doesn't have to be. Think about this discouraging fact: When trading stocks, you can be right 90 percent of the time and go broke. Conversely, think about another all too encouraging little fact: When trading stocks, you can make mistakes 90 percent of the time and still amass a fortune. Sounds like a great business to be in, doesn't it? Well, unfortunately, the latter is not a business strategy I can wholeheartedly recommend. Still, odd and amazing as this second fact may seem, there is a very important lesson in it. Not only must you immediately admit your mistakes, you must then strive to minimize the cost of these mistakes. Unfortunately, many would-be traders never even learn the first part of this lesson.

The inability to admit mistakes is no rare malady among prospective stock traders. It is a virulent, deadly plague. I hope you noticed that I said "among prospective" stock traders. I did not say "among successful stock traders," or even "long-term stock traders" because prospective stock traders who do not learn to admit to their mistakes, do not stay solvent long enough to become successful or long-term traders. The simple cure for this malady is to force yourself to look at the numbers, figure out their effect on your balance sheet, and then, if necessary, reign in your ego long enough to admit to your mistakes. The next and final step is to act as quickly as possible to cut your losses.

Minimizing the cost of subsequent mistakes is, for many people, much easier than admitting them after the fact. The surest way to do so is to devise an exit strategy even before you enter a position on a stock. For example, you are sure the stock Helium Balloons Unlimited is going to go up. If you weren't sure, I choose to believe you would not buy it. In any case, if you are so sure, at the same time you buy it long, make up your mind to sell it if the stock price drops even ¼ below your cost. Sure, you may lose this ¼ in the blink of an eye, but you won't lose any more than ¼. An automatic stop loss order would be even better. Not only does this make it unnecessary to depend on your attention span and reflexes, it guards against a far more serious threat, interference from your ego.

In case I have not as yet made my point, allow me one more chance to impress on you the importance of cutting your losses. Let's say some idiot, not you of course, decides the best thing he can do with his money is use it to make even more money trading stocks. What could be simpler? Well the answer happens to be a different book, much longer than this one. Lacking the time and space to get into that now, let's just get back to our idiot. We will assume that, like you, he or she can read. And that, like you, he had the foresight, or dumb luck, to buy *Technical Trading Online*. In fact he even, like you, read up to this page. That means he read and took to heart Rule 1. Ah, if I could only, with confidence, add "like you" to this last sentence.

On his first daring move, our hero takes a one-hundred share position long on a can't miss stock with a stop set ¼ below cost. When his stock heads in the wrong direction, the automatic stop closes him out. He takes another position long on another great-looking stock. Unfortunately, this position ends the same way as the first. So do his next fourteen positions in a row. Thanks to the automatic stops, ignoring commissions and other costs, our boy has lost only $200. Now he might not have learned anything from this experience, but I'm sure that by then you would have. At a minimum, this beating would have convinced you to suspend trading until you at least tried to finish the rest of this book. And the beauty of this lesson is that the most this beating could have cost you is $200.

Enough real-life adventures, for now at least. The strategies and safeguards for cutting your losses when selling short are similar to those for buying long. We will get into specifics for both later in the book.

rule 2   let your profits run

Rule 1 concerned cutting your losses. Well cutting losses is not quite enough. I have never met anyone who traded stocks with the objective of cutting his or her losses. Face it, the best way to cut your losses, ignoring inflation, is to bury your money in the backyard (preferably at night, preferably when there's no moon, but that too is another book, perhaps my next). Cutting your losses is a good defense, but if you are not offensive-minded, trading stocks is not for you.

Let's assume, for simplicity's sake, you always trade stocks in blocks of one hundred shares. Let's also assume, for reality's sake, that thanks to automatic stops, you only lost ¼ on each of the first eight stocks you bought long. Ignoring commissions and other costs, your ninth stock needs only to rise two points to get you even. Getting even may be satisfying enough where ex-marital partners are concerned, but it does not get the job done when trading stocks. Take my word for it, you will need every ¼ point profit you can get.

Technical Trading Online will teach you how to let your profits run until you have squeezed your stocks like a lemon. It will help you learn to recognize ahead of time the events you should be prepared for while holding a long or short position. You will end up with a sure sense of when to move your stops and how tight to set them.

rule 3   trade with the trend

Have you ever tried swimming against a current? It may be great exercise, but it's no prescription for making progress. In fact, if the current is moving faster than you can swim, it is a sure-fire prescription for drowning. Similarly, trading against the trend, especially for the novice, is a pretty good prescription for insolvency.

Let's say you have found a stock that you are confident is ready for a surge in price. Almost the entire market is losing points, and this stock is holding its own. The question is: Why shouldn't you buy it?

The answer is: Who needs a stock that is going sideways? It is difficult for traders to gain or retain confidence in a particular stock when they have been drained, however temporarily, of their confidence in the market as a whole. Confidence is contagious, but pessimism can be a virulent epidemic. If a stock is holding its own in a falling market, it is not only a good bet that it will rise in an up market, it is a good investment.

The trick is not to commit your capital until it can earn a return. You want to buy the stock just before or after it starts to rise. How can you be sure when that will be? You can't. However, a damn good indication of an imminent rise in the stock would be an actual rise in the market. Of course, other conditions and indicators should be taken into consideration, but the most compelling indicator should be the direction of the market as a whole.

There are respected strategies for taking positions against the trend, but I feel they should be left to the experienced, expert trader. If you, as a novice, insist on trying some of these strategies, I strongly suggest you restrict your source of capital to currently earned profits. This, for the immediate future, should prevent you from taking any substantial positions against the trend.

To trade with the trend, it is helpful to be able to recognize a trend. I do not recommend the Dow Jones Industrial Average as a primary indicator. It is an average of only 30 stocks, while the New York Stock Exchange lists approximately 3,000 stocks. The Dow Jones can and sometimes does mask the actual market trend. We will go much deeper into this subject later in the book. We will also cover the various indicators that will help you not only identify a trend, but also, of even more value, predict a change in trend.

I have tried to convince you, using cold logic, to always trade with the trend. Let's face it, cold logic is not as effective as it used to be, and probably never was. So if you are more susceptible to marketing jingles or New Age homilies, perhaps some warm, catchy, upbeat words will be more effective:

"Trade with the trend. The trend is your friend."

Try chanting these sentences during trading breaks. If you can, blurt them out instead of curse words. You may find that these deceptively simple words, if repeated often enough, will gain religious force. However, I wouldn't chant them too loud. Proselytizing can make you one unpopular stock trader.

rule 4   never average down your losing positions

Let us assume you get a hot tip about Lead Balloons Ltd. Share price is sure to double to $200 by the end of the week. Luckily, you are able to dive for your keyboard in time to pick up 100,000 shares at a mere cost of only $100 dollars a share, and a dislocated index finger. By the time you relocate your index finger, Lead Balloons has unfathomably dropped 10 points. If you would have waited a few more minutes, you could have bought it at $90. $200 minus $90 would have left you with an eventual per share profit of $110 when Balloons reaches its $200 potential. Still, this is no time to be greedy. Your $100 per share profit will be good enough. Even when Balloons subsequently drops to $80, you decide not to cry over spilt milk. Admittedly, you do feel a twinge of envy a few minutes later when one of your friends buys in at only $70 a share. That means she will eventually reap a $130 profit, almost 200 percent. That's double yours. Pity.

However, when Balloons drops to $45, a slight loss of confidence causes you to recheck your information. To your relief, not only does your source stand by his original tip, he is now positive that the stock will reach $250. Sure enough, less than two days later, Balloons rallies from $45 to $50.

If the stock was a bargain at $100, it is surely twice the bargain now. Besides, buying a stock for $100 and selling it for $50 is not the way to get rich, at least as far as you can figure out. Another thing, that 50 percent drop in share price is not going to look good in your accounts. However, if you scoop up another 100,000 shares at $50, your average drop in stock value is miraculously cut in half to only 25 percent. This will make your eventual profits look even better. Besides, then the stock price need only rise to $75 instead of $100 for you to break even.

Not only do you scoop up the extra 100,000 at $50, you eventually pick up an additional 200,000 share blocks at $40, $30, $20, and $10. Unfortunately and unfathomably, shortly thereafter, Lead Balloons Ltd. goes broke. Still, you have managed to reduce your average price paid per share from $100 to $35. To your surprise, as an added bonus, you suddenly realize that you have purchased all outstanding shares. That's right, Lead Balloons is all yours, lock, stock, and barrel. And as if that bountiful bonus weren't enough, the barrel happens to be a perfect fit.

However, despite how well things worked out, I think you now understand that ending up with that barrel was due more to luck than to skill. Let us hope you never again break Rule 4 by averaging down your losing positions.

Psychology, and of course we are referring to the pop variety, sells books. So now is the perfect time to include some in *Technical Trading Online*. Unsuccessful traders invariably lack one or both of two essential attributes—knowledge and discipline.

You can pick up a good chunk of knowledge by reading this book, and do so relatively painlessly. Yet, as much as it hurts my ego to admit it, neither this book nor any other will, by itself, give you sufficient knowledge to become a successful stock trader. It can only arm you with enough background and strategies to give you a fighting chance to stay alive and active in the market long enough to gain knowledge and turn yourself into a successful trader. You must remain determined to add to your store of knowledge, however vast you may judge it to be, every single day, including days when the market is closed.

Discipline is a trait you must develop for yourself. Reinforce and strengthen whatever discipline you already possess, until you are sure that, no matter how stressful the crisis or how euphoric the mood, you retain enough discipline to hold sway over your emotions and ego. If you lack discipline and are incapable of developing some, forget about trading stocks. In fact, stop reading at the end of this sentence, and try to take this book back to the store for a refund.

In the stock market, everyone makes mistakes. Mistakes mean losses, the financial type. Discipline helps you push your ego aside, and admit to making a mistake. In the stock market, the cost of mistakes is money. The sooner you can admit to mistakes and act accordingly, the less those mistakes will cost you. Costs decrease or eliminate profits. Discipline lowers these costs and protects profits, *if* you have profits. At the very least, discipline lowers costs.

I have already admitted that this book does not contain all the knowledge you will need to be a successful stock trader. I have also more or less admitted that I cannot teach you the discipline you will need, only the reasons that you will need it. Now here comes the real killer. Neither I, nor anyone else, can teach you the right way to trade stocks. Fortunately or unfortunately, there is no right way. Each trader's methodology is as different as his or her DNA and upbringing. The purpose of *Technical Trading Online* is to familiarize you with the many tools available. You will have to choose among these tools and among the ways they can be used.

summary

This chapter should have added to your knowledge. I hope you can develop the discipline to abide by the four rules it contains. Let's go over them one more time. Trading with the trend involves the necessary knowledge to identify the trend and the discipline to resist bucking it. Cutting your losses is almost pure discipline. Letting your profits run involves both knowledge and discipline. Never averaging down your losses is nothing but discipline.

I have used cold logic and even a little jingle in trying to convey the importance of these rules. Now I will try something else—cold fear. The following is a true story. Let it be a lesson to you.

Once upon a time there was a very big and well respected company called Capital Management. The capital under its management was roughly $100 billion—a sum sizable enough to impress anyone outside of Congress. Capital Management managed to lose $95 billion of this little nest egg. How? Not for lack of knowledge. Company employees had plenty of that. They were the darlings of Wall Street. They put down sensible positions based on sound knowledge. Yet they started to incur losses.

Did they follow Rule 1 and cut their losses? No, they did the opposite and broke Rule 4. They added to these positions to average down their losses. As if that weren't enough, they broke Rule 3 and traded against the trend.

Individual traders have done quite well with mere fractions of Capital Management's knowledge. What Capital Management lacked was discipline. The only one of the Four Golden Rules of Stock Trading that they did not break was Rule 2. Unfortunately, they did not really obey Rule 2 either. To let your profits run, it is essential that you have profits in the first place.

chapter 2

the Kinematic Model

price/earnings ratios? this ain't your father's stock market

As I mentioned, price/earnings ratios and the other traditional ways of valuing a company's stock do surprisingly little to explain price movement in today's markets. In this chapter, I take on that task by constructing a general, idealized model of this price movement.

The only way to make money in the stock market is to take a position. Before you take a position on a particular stock, you have to figure out the trend of the market as a whole, the strength of this trend, and decide if it will continue or reverse. Once you have decided, you must apply Rule 3, Trade with the Trend. To illustrate exactly how trends come into play, we construct a *Kinematic Model*.

The Kinematic Model in Figure 2.1 could represent an index such as the S&P 500, but we use it to represent individual

figure 2.1   the Kinematic Model

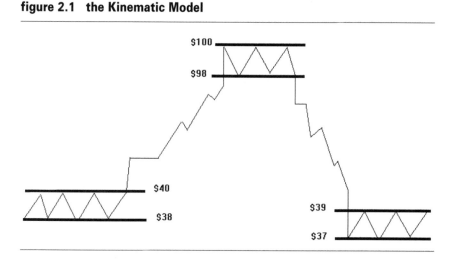

stocks. Though it will prove extremely useful as a teaching and learning tool, please don't mistake it for a perfect representation of the behavior of all stocks or any particular stock under all situations. That is far from the case. This theoretical model is not built on any strict laws of science or nature. A quick look at the actual stock market will provide many exceptions to it. We use this model merely to illustrate what you should look for and how you should react to what you see, and also to quicken these reactions, making them almost reflexive. Furthermore, this Kinematic Model will be used in conjunction with other market indicators we discuss in later chapters.

I have mentioned before that no two traders trade exactly alike. Likewise, no two people make the exact same use of this model. Take from it what you can, and leave only what you must.

In general, stocks go through four phases:

1. Accumulation
2. Price markup
3. Distribution
4. Price markdown

Figure 2.1 is an idealization of this behavior using a hypothetical stock, Amalgamated Banks and Casinos. The thin line represents price variations of this stock. The thicker parallel lines represent trading ranges.

Assume there are one million shares of Amalgamated outstanding. The $38 to $40 trading range on the left of Figure 2.1 represents the accumulation by institutional and other large investors of 900,000 shares. Those investors, believing that the company will do well and that the price will rise, were always there ready to buy up the supply when Amalgamated dropped to $38. Some of them kept buying until the price reached $40. Then they would wait for the price to drop again, ready to buy up more shares. They have taken 90 percent of the outstanding shares of this stock out of the marketplace. This leaves only 100,000 shares available. The institutions and people who have accumulated the stock can only be enticed to sell it by a healthy profit, which means a higher stock price.

Remember that this accumulation phase means the withholding of supply from the marketplace. New demand eventually comes up against reduced supply, ending the accumulation phase and starting the price markup phase. Demand is now greater than supply, so the stock price rises from $40 all the way up to $100. A large percentage of the stock holders who have taken this pleasantly profitable ride are now either satisfied with their profits or believe that the stock price has finished its upward movement. They decide to sell and take their profits, ending the price markup phase.

Renewed supply coming into the market begins the distribution phase. The price slips down to $98, spurring new demand. This drives the price back up to $100. Supply and demand being roughly equal, Amalgamated rises and falls a few more times within this distribution price range of $98 to $100.

Finally, there comes a time when the supply still coming onto the market exhausts the demand. The price markdown phase begins when demand no longer swallows up all the supply. At this point, with supply greater than demand, the price of Amalgamated drops.

Now, let's go back and take another, closer look at our Kinematic Model. This model is divided into four phases:

1. An accumulation phase where stock price fluctuates between $38 and $40

2. A price markup phase in which the price moves up from $40 to $100

3. A distribution phase where the price fluctuates between $98 and $100

4. A price markdown phase in which the price drops to $37

What are the characteristics of an accumulation phase? First of all, price fluctuates within a trading range—in our particular model between $38 and $40. Yet this phase looks very similar to the distribution phase where the stock price fluctuates between $98 and $100. There is no reason why an accumulation phase cannot also occur within a $98 to $100 range. So what is the difference between these two phases? The difference is that during an accumulation phase, large investors are taking shares off the market in anticipation of a price rise. During a distribution phase, they are returning these shares to the marketplace and taking their profits.

How can we be positive which phase we are in? There is only one sure way—if we ourselves are doing the accumulating or distributing. The next best way is to be in possession of unimpeachable information. Even if there really is such a thing, in this case unimpeachable probably means indictable, which often means incarceration and *always* means the equally distasteful business of consorting with lawyers. Yet there are tools, methods, and even tricks for making a very educated, unindictable guess. *Technical Trading Online* familiarizes you with the most worthwhile of these.

Why is it important to know the difference between an accumulation and a distribution phase? Because their outcomes are opposite. The likely outcome of an accumulation phase is a price markup phase—the time for the stock trader to buy long.

The likely outcome of a distribution phase is a price markdown phase—time for a trader to sell short.

At the end of the accumulation phase, demand outstrips supply creating an upward price trend. The successful stock trader must understand the psychology behind this trend in the same way a chess player must understand the psychology behind his opponent's moves. Look at Figure 2.2, Point 14. By the time the stock price has risen to this point, it has caught the eye of a large number of traders. Most of them are regretting not buying in at Points 10 and 13, not to mention Point 8. However, this does not prevent them from hesitating once again. By the time Amalgamated rises to Point 16, these traders are really kicking themselves. Every time the stock has risen, pent-up demand has increased. The small decrease in price that ends at Point 17 is just too much of an enticement for

figure 2.2   waypoints on the Kinematic Model

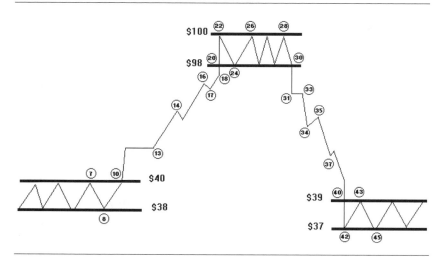

many of these traders. They dive into the market in a rush, taking others along with them.

A significant number of traders were reckless enough to buck the trend. Maybe they thought they had some inside information, exclusive insight, or perhaps they saw no sane relationship between Amalgamated's balance sheet and its price rise. These skeptics have been selling short all along the way, waiting greedily for Amalgamated to crash. Whatever alibi they have for its continued rise, you can bet they are getting nervous, very nervous. At Point 18, the short sellers have had enough. They rush to buy in order to cover their shorts. Their buying, in combination with that fueled by pent-up demand, shoots Amalgamated's stock price up into a buying climax (Point 22). This last, precipitous rise is characterized by a wide price spread and huge volume.

Now the pent-up demand, by definition, is no longer pent up. It's spent. Once the traders who bucked the trend have already covered their shorts, this source of demand has also evaporated. How can demand keep from decreasing? It can't, at least not in our Kinematic Model. Satisfied traders taking their profits start to provide supply. Supply being greater than demand, Amalgamated's price slips down from $100 to $98 at Point 24. Let's call this point the *Reaction After Climax*. This reduced stock price attracts new buyers, confident Amalgamated's price rise will continue. They raise the price back up to $100, the former high, at Point 26. If the stock price breaks through to a new high, it just may keep on going. More likely, as our model illustrates, this is merely a test of the previous high (Point 22). Amalgamated slips back down to $98. This slight drop proves enticing enough to draw in some more buyers, who figure the stall in share price is just a consolidation. They drive the stock back up to $100 at Point 28.

Connecting Points 22 and 26, and extrapolating this line forward, gives us a *resistance line*. Drawing a line parallel to the resistance line and through the Reaction After Climax (Point 24) gives us a *support line*. Between the resistance and support lines, you now have a distribution trading range of $98 to $100.

Usually, after a few more unsuccessful tests of the resistance line, sellers begin to outnumber buyers. The market comes to believe that a new high in the near future is unlikely. It should not be any surprise to you that since supply then exceeds demand, share price falls. In the case of our model, it falls through the support line at Point 30. With this critical psychological barrier broken, it free falls all the way to Point 31.

We have now reached the place in our model where the psychology behind it becomes most interesting, especially if your interest is stimulated by bloodshed. The ancient Greeks believed that one of the necessary aspects of tragedy had to be the hero's fall from a very high place. If it has not already been written, some day a doctoral candidate with an interest in the Classics and assets in the stock market, will write a thesis insisting that the high place the Greeks had in mind was a stock's distribution phase. And it would not surprise me if someday someone unearths a long-lost Shakespeare tragedy about a star-crossed stock trader. I guarantee you that this play's last act will occur during a price markdown phase.

It would not take much of a writer to milk the drama inherent in Point 34 or 37 on the Kinematic Model. Our hero would be the starry-eyed schmoe who entered the market just below Point 30. Instead of selling short when the support line collapsed, he smelled a short-term aberration and a bargain stock that was sure to recover and smash the $100 resistance line on its way up into the stratosphere. Well, he smelled wrong. By the time our schmoe regains his sense of smell, Amalgamated

Banks and Casinos has hit Point 34, giving off a rather sickening aroma. Though his hot stock has dropped 20 points since its purchase, there is hope in his heart as it then shoots up a whole quarter, then another eighth. He was right all the time. He is sure of it. And as our boy watches with more confidence, the price rises another eighth. Just to make sure the recovery continues, he takes time for a little prayer, "Thank you, God. If you just let me out of this mess, I'll never again break the Third Golden Rule. No, Lord, this sinner will never again trade against the trend."

Sure enough, God answers his prayer, temporarily that is, and Amalgamated goes up another ⅛, to Point 35. Unfortunately, this was just one of those feeble little rallies with its bright, brief ray of hope illuminating a dark path down to despair and destruction. And as our hero watches his stock price plunge, he remembers exactly what he ate for lunch, every little morsel. Doing so is easy. It is all on the way back up. With not a second to spare, he makes it into the bathroom and finds himself praying to another god, a porcelain one. He holds on to that toilet with all his strength, as if it were anchored upon the spinning, wave-washed deck of a fragile little ship tossed mercilessly by hurricane driven seas.

Against all odds, our hero weathers the storm and survives. He stops at the mirror on his way out of the bathroom, making an ineffective, half-hearted attempt to overhaul his appearance. Walking toward his monitors, he prays silently, "Please God, let there be a rally. Let me out of this position, and I promise to change my ways."

"No deal," says God. Amalgamated is now on its way down to Point 37. Our boy can neither eat nor sleep. All he can do is drink coffee, which helps to explain why he can neither eat nor sleep. He watches the stock's price sink, taking no solace in what should be a comforting fact: From the look of his monitors, our schmoe is not alone. There are thousand of idiots out there, just like him.

Finally, he decides to face up to his mistake, to do what he should have done 30 points ago. Our hero decides to bite the bullet and bail out on his supposed bargain. Then, like an answered prayer, just as he is about to do so, Amalgamated hits Point 37 and starts to recover. Covering his position in Heaven, though unfortunately not on earth, our boy gives thanks to God. For a little more insurance, he takes out his checkbook and starts to write a generous contribution to the Salvation Army. However, before he can sign the check, the bottom drops out of the market for Amalgamated Banks and Casinos. His fellow investors, gutless thousands of them, just couldn't take the heat anymore. The pressure was too much. They bailed out whether they had parachutes or not. Selling almost simultaneously, they drive the stock price nearly straight down in a selling climax characterized by a wide, wide price range and high, high volume. Our hero, beaten down in despair, staggers after the *hoi polloi* and closes out his own position.

Prospective stock traders, remember this: Even in tragedy there can be solace. Now, at least the pressure is off. Our hero and his comrades find relief in the fact that, even despite the verdict, at least their trial is over. Our boy calmly leaves the office, telling himself that today he has really learned something, which is not an everyday occurrence. Now, instead of writing a check to the Salvation Army, he is on his way there for supper, by foot. Our hero is at peace with himself. Maybe he just wasn't cut out to be a stock trader. Maybe he should look for a less stressful occupation. He pictures himself in a Santa Claus suit, ringing a bell next to a Salvation Army kettle. There is a beatific smile on Santa's face, and also on his own. The Santa job seems appealing, almost idyllic, especially compared to trading stocks.

Dear Reader, the previous paragraphs are not pure fantasy, or even pure fiction. I know well of what I speak, from personal experience. Yes, your esteemed author has made similar mistakes. This book is written to save you the painful experience of doing the same. Just follow my four little oft-repeated rules. In case you have forgotten, I'll list them again. In case you haven't, read them anyway. The Four Golden Rules of Stock Trading:

1. Cut your losses.
2. Let your profits run.
3. Trade with the trend.
4. Never average down your losing positions.

Now that we have all promised ourselves not to repeat the mistakes of our departed hero, let us buy for almost nothing his new nineteen inch monitors and return to the market. The first things we notice are some interesting occurrences that have happened since his tragic downfall. When the selling climax ended at Point 42, supply was just about exhausted. Anyone who had been inclined to sell either did so or got trampled to death in the rush to do so, thus leaving his or her stock tied up in probate until the next Ice Age. Demand may still be weak, but cannot be as weak as supply, not on the high side of Chapter 11 it can't. Amalgamated Banks and Casinos, like a phoenix, rises from the ashes. Well, perhaps more like a drugged walrus. You see, there were some smart traders, previous readers of this very book no doubt, who had decided to trade with the trend. They shorted at Point 33, or even Point 30. Now, judging correctly that Amalgamated's price won't drop any lower than $37, or perhaps merely deciding not to get greedy, they cover their shorts. Also, there are those traders who see no long-term change in Amalgamated's prospects despite the drop in stock price. They and other traders, for various reasons, judge Amalgamated a bargain. Demand picks up and so does share price, to $39 at Point 43. Let's call this point the Rally After Climax.

No rally can last forever, and a Rally After Climax rarely—very rarely—comes even close to lasting forever. There are always some pure-bred short sellers out there, convinced Amalgamated is on its way to Chapter 11. There are also some of those buyers who entered at Point 42 looking for a little bump. They got it and are satisfied to take their profits. So share price drops back down to $37 at Point 45, at the same time testing the resistance line. The resistance line passes this test, and what do you know? We have got ourselves another trading range.

So now, while Amalgamated is caught within a trading range, it's time to find another, more active stock, or better yet, time to take a short break.

At the risk of shocking you, perhaps out of a reader's stupor, let me state that the Kinematic Model is just that, a model. If you cannot fathom this as plain logic, please accept it as a leap of faith. Real stocks in real markets during a distribution phase *will not fit* our model exactly. However, you may be surprised by how close they can come. Another thing to keep in mind, the Kinematic Model is more easily applicable to weekly and daily charts than it is to five-minute charts.

In case our model is wearing you out, let me try to lengthen your attention span by reminding you why you are reading this book: It certainly isn't for the "juice," no more than you should be trading stocks for the "juice." No, this book is for people who want to trade stocks for profit, which in this book means *financial profit.* Understanding our Kinematic Model will help you acquire these profits. Stocks can do three things: go up, go down, or remain unchanged. When they are going to go up, you want to buy long. When they are going to go down, you want to sell short. When they aren't going anywhere, you want to go somewhere else before their tight trading ranges mesmerize you.

Our model, when applied to an actual stock, is an indicator of what that stock will do. It teaches you how to look at the stock and what to look for. It trains you to take a judgmental approach by showing you what evidence to weigh. It enables you to make more informed decisions and find more compelling reasons to enter positions and, when necessary, abandon them. You will be able to systematize your trading, thus reducing the uncertainty and the stress that can accompany it. Once you have taken a reasoned position, you will then have the confidence and conviction to act quickly, unflinchingly, and forcefully to either support or abandon that position.

Over time, your reactions will become not only more effective, but also more reflexive. They need to. Evander Hollyfield couldn't stop and prepare a strategy for every punch Mike Tyson threw at him. Most of Hollyfield's strategy should have been taken care of before he entered the ring. The rest should have been worked out between rounds. When Tyson's left hook was on its way, there was no time for Hollyfield to strategize: "Let me see. The conditions are as follows. Tyson's left hook is one foot from my noggin. My options are—" If Hollyfield ever did resume this train of thought, it would probably be from a hospital bed. No, this was no time to strategize; it was time to react. Studying our model, then applying it thoughtfully and judiciously to your daily trading, will improve both your understanding and reaction time. Don't ever assume it will make you bulletproof. Hell, it won't even make you teeth proof. Anyone who enters the market, no matter how exceptional his or her strategy, knowledge, and discipline, is always at risk, and from directions and weapons that can and will be surprising. Forget this fact, and you may lose more than a piece of your ear. Evander Hollyfield still has all the equipment necessary to sit down.

That said, let's see if we can use the Kinematic Model to make some money. Look at Figure 2.3. What do we see between Points 1 and 10? Not just a trading range, but also an accumulation phase. What do we see between Points 20 and 30? Another trading range, but this time it encompasses a distribution phase. Despite their opposite outcomes, both phases sure look similar. An accumulation phase's most likely resolution is up, a price markup phase. A distribution phase's most likely resolution is down, a price markdown phase. So toward the end of an accumulation phase, you should be looking for buy long signals. Toward the end of a distribution phase, you should be looking for sell short signals.

figure 2.3 buy signals

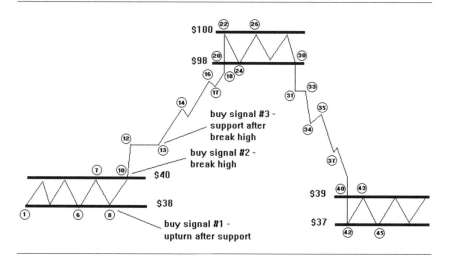

Take a closer look at the accumulation phase. At Point 7, the support line has withstood three tests. You should at least be thinking about buying on support. The resistance line has also withstood three tests, but because this is an accumulation phase, it is a good bet that this resistance will eventually be broken. There is another good bet about how it will be broken.

Say you are walking down the street one morning when you hear a scream. It comes from a house with smoke pouring out a window. What do you do? That's right, you check your watch to see if you have enough time before the market opens. By chance, you do. Of course the windows are too high to reach, and the doors are all locked. The screaming continues. You check your watch again. If you are going to make the market's opening, you had better break down the door and do it fast. You slam your shoulder into the door. It holds. You do it again, meeting the same resistance. You continue to slam your shoulder into the door. The feel of impact tells you something is about to give and hopefully it won't be your collar bone. Sure enough, on your next try, the door flies open and you fly in after it. There was no way you could have stopped yourself for a precautionary sniff at the threshold. No, by now you are inside, way inside, eating smoke. The force needed to break open the door and the sudden removal of resistance propelled you forward with added momentum. This is exactly what happens at Point 10 on our model. Point 8, if not Point 6, had been our first buy signal, and our next one, just past Point 10 and called the *Break High,* is a far, far stronger signal—resistance has been broken and momentum is propelling share price higher. Even if you bought at Point 8, this is a good time to buy again.

What then should you do between Points 12 and 13? That depends on exactly what type of trader you are. Chapter 6 is devoted solely to a discussion of this subject. In the meantime, let it suffice to say that there are four main types of traders. Their defining, though not sole characteristic, is the timeframe within which they hold their positions. The day trader can easily take and abandon 50 stock positions in a day, some of them lasting seconds and none extending overnight. The overnight trader usually buys his stocks in the afternoon and sells them all before lunch the next day. The swing trader will usually keep his positions from a few days to a few weeks. The position trader buys stocks with the intention of keeping them for at least a few weeks.

Returning to our model, many of those traders who bought in between Point 8 and Point 12 are day traders and overnight traders. They are quite willing to take their profits now. Should they be? If they are pure day and overnight traders, they certainly should be. Their style is to move in and out of trends such as this numerous times. The position trader has no intention of taking his profits until he judges the stock to be in or close to its distribution phase. The swing trader is another story. If he thinks Point 12 is the start of a reaction, a drop in price, then he should take his profits and climb back aboard as soon as the uptrend resumes. In hindsight, there proved to be no point in this. However, if hindsight did not always come too late, it would be called foresight. The decision to sell could have been quite judicious at the time. Here we have the market moving sideways in a consolidation. For those intending to hold on, a small drop in price would also be acceptable. The lateral movement ends in an upturn just after Point 13. This is our third buy signal.

Remember our first buy signal was at Point 8, if not Point 6, both points of support. You may have bought at Point 7 because you thought, wrongly in the case of our model, that Point 7 would be the Break High, or because you were confident, rightly in the case of our model, that even if the price dropped to Point 8, it would rise back again to $40, the line of resistance, and the trading range would continue.

You can see from the Kinematic Model that it is wise, when buying on support, to wait for some slight confirmation that stock price is starting back up. Therefore, our first buy signal should come just after and above Points 6 or 8. Furthermore, watch your stock closely as it approaches Points 7 and 10. If you bought at Point 6, it is usually wise to take your small profit just as share price starts to drop again, right after Point 7, even if (and because) you are sure the price will bounce back up again to Point 10. Just be alert and ready to buy in again right after the upturn at Point 8.

There is another very important reason to wait for a slight upturn before buying on support, as Figure 2.4 illustrates. To help you remember it, we will give this phenomenon an indelible name: the Shakeout-Fake-Out-Before-the-Breakout. Don't

figure 2.4   sell signals

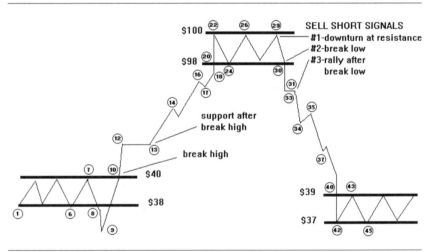

for a second forget that you are not the only drooling, overconfident genius who has discovered this trading range and who is buying on support and selling on resistance. You may also be among those who have stop loss orders just below the line of support. Let's say, as sometimes happens, a very slight break in support at Point 8 sets off some of these stops, thus increasing supply just enough to cause another slight drop in share price. Now, instead of share price recovering, the additional drop sets off more stops, dropping the share price further, and so on until all stops have been activated and a precipitous fall in share price ends at Point 9.

Notice, however, that stock price recovers. The Break High still occurs at Point 10, as if the Shakeout-Fake-Out-Before-the Breakout hadn't even happened. Unfortunately for you, if you had set an automatic stop, the Shakeout-Fake-Out knocked you off your rocketing stock way before it even recovered to $38. Clearly it would have been better for you to have placed a mental stop, but in all honesty you may have activated it yourself anyway. In any case, the sooner your stop was activated, the less your loss. And if you were smart enough to continue monitoring the stock, you could have jumped back on very soon after Point 9. This would have not only made you an extra few bucks, it would have saved you some mental wear and tear between Points 8 and 9.

How can you be positive that a precipitous price drop toward Point 9 is merely a temporary price aberration to be calmly weathered, a Shakeout-Fake-Out. You can't, not positively. However, when you see a similar occurrence involving a real stock, check the volume, and check it fast. You won't have much time to act, if action is in fact necessary. A very large price drop and very small volume is a good, though not foolproof indication of a Shakeout-Fake-Out-Before-the-Breakout. If you do bail out, and even if you don't, you may want to follow the stock price down with an automatic buy stop order just above it. We will discuss this entry strategy later.

In review, return to Figure 2.3. Our first buy signals—signals to buy on support—occur at Point 6 or 8, or better yet, just after them at the slightest confirmation of an uptrend. Our second and superior buy signal, the Break High, occurs just past Point 10. Now our third buy signal, Support After Break High, occurs at Point 13. These are the three buy signals you should watch for at the end of an accumulation phase.

Monitoring a distribution trading range is a similar exercise, as illustrated in Figure 2.4. At Point 29, the resistance line has already been tested a few times. Chances are it will outlast the support line in the near future. So just after Point 29, when Amalgamated's price starts on its way down again, can you be fairly confident it will fall at least to or close to the support line? You can, and you should recognize this point as Sell Signal 1—sell short just after the point of resistance.

Now we come to Point 30 and the opportunity for another brilliant metaphor. Think of the support line as ice on a lake. You are skating along and the ice seems fine. You decide to test it with a jump. Sure enough, there's support. It holds for another jump, and one more. Then you just happen to see that good-looking new face in town smiling right at you. You return the smile and explode into the air with by far your highest jump of the day. Bad move. The ice cracks. Ice water is no support at all. You don't just go down to your knees, or your waist, or even your neck. No, thanks to your shiny new skates and soaking wet clothing, you sink, way, way over your head, right down to the cold, muddy lake bottom. Something very similar happens at Point 30. You should sell short at the break in support, which we refer to as the *Break Low*—Sell Signal 2.

Sell Signal 3 is just after Point 33, the Rally After Break Low. In this case, Point 31 to Point 33 is more of a consolidation than a rally, but the drop in price after Point 33 confirms the downtrend. Remember, Sell Signal 1 was at the resistance point. Sell Signal 2 was at the break in support. Let me repeat: It is far easier to locate these points on a weekly or daily chart, than on a five-minute chart where they are even more valuable. Among other things, it's a case of not being able to see the forest for the trees.

There is another important phenomenon to keep in mind. Remember the Shakeout-Fake-Out-Before-the-Breakout at the end of the accumulation phase? As indicated in Figure 2.5a, something very similar sometimes occurs at the end of the distribution phase. Because of its importance, we shall give it another indelible name—the Shake-Up-Fake-Out-Before-the-Breakdown.

If you see the break in resistance and wide price spread indicative of the Shake-Up-Fake-Out-Before-the-Breakdown, immediately, and I do mean immediately, check stock volume.

figure 2.5   price markup and markdown phases

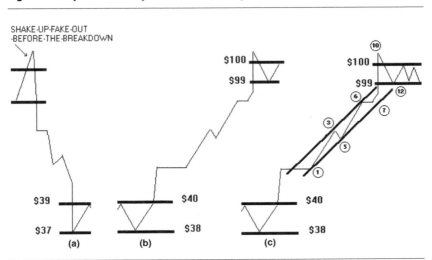

Very low volume would tend to confirm a Shake-Up-Fake-Out. It could have been caused by short covering, hitting buy stop orders, or both. As with the Shakeout-Fake-Out-Before-the-Breakout, you may want to follow the stock price, this time with automatic sell short stop orders.

Another thing to keep in mind is that in a markdown phase, you usually have less time to locate the mentioned points and their associated sell signals compared to the buy signals on a markup phase. Markdown phases tend to be strikingly more precipitous than markup phases. One of the reasons for this is that greed helps fuel uptrends and fear helps fuel downtrends. Greed can be tempered by an extremely common deficiency, that of guts. Fear is reinforced and accelerated by this very same deficiency. Thus, fear is by far the stronger emotion. Another reason markdown phases are more precipitous than markup phases is the confusion inherent in both of these phases. Confusion during a markup phase tends to decelerate it. Conversely, confusion during a markdown phase tends to accelerate it.

The high-rising markup phases and fast-falling markdown phases that connect trading ranges can also be thought of as *trends.* If you are going to think about them, you might as well know how to draw them. Figure 2.5b is an uptrend. Figure 2.5c illustrates how to mark the bottom of the first two troughs (Points 1 and 5), connect these two points, and extrapolate them forward to draw a support line. Now draw a line parallel to the support line and through the highest point of the rally between the two troughs (Point 3). This is the resistance line. We will frequently refer to it as an overbought line because a price rise caused by "overbuying" is likely to lead to profit taking. You will see this pattern very often, even on five-minute charts. In an uptrend like this, you want to buy, not sell short.

And you want to buy immediately after a pullback, that is, immediately after the last point of support.

Let's assume you take a position just after Point 5 in Figure 2.5c. Sure enough, share price rises to Point 6. Then, it moves almost laterally but drops slightly to Point 7. Smart trader that you are, you originally set a stop below Point 5. If you would have moved it up to just below Point 6 to follow the rising price, the almost lateral movement between Points 6 and 7 might have activated and closed you out before that mouth-watering rise between Points 7 and 10. This would not have happened if you had moved the stop parallel to and just below the extrapolated support line.

Before we say *au revoir* to Figure 2.5c, notice that our stock enters a trading range at Point 12. Unfortunately, this range is too narrow to offer a worthwhile profit. Unless you have a very good idea where share price is going when it breaks out of this trading range, I would advise you not to get entranced by its tiny ups and downs. Check back periodically to see if this stock breaks its range, but in the meantime, take your profits and find a more interesting, less mesmerizing stock to concentrate on.

Figure 2.6a is a downtrend. Not only does it look like the opposite of an uptrend, for our purposes we treat it as such. In Figure 2.6b, we have connected the first two rally peaks to make a resistance line. We then draw a line parallel to it, through the lowest point in the trough between them. Again, though this is commonly called a support line, we will frequently refer to it as an *oversold line*. The precipitous price drop is attributed to overselling, and will likely generate short covering and bargain hunting, thus an accompanying price recovery. During a downtrend, you want to sell short, and do so on the last point of supply.

figure 2.6   downtrends

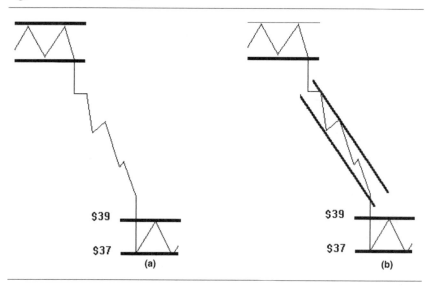

Let's take a closer look at an uptrend such as that in Figure 2.5c. Day traders will often see mini-buying climaxes such as at Point 10 on five-minute charts. Now from Point 1 to Point 7, you had a normal, balanced interaction between supply and demand. The sudden parabolic rise to Point 10 indicates that the relationship between supply and demand has swung to an extreme, or in more technical terms, gone kaplooey. So as not to depress you, let's assume that you had the foresight to buy long around Point 1 at $60. And let's assume the break in resistance leading to Point 10 was caused by a burst of covering shorts, a likely assumption.

Unless you like losing money, you had your exit strategy planned even before you entered the market. The simplest strategy involves a stop order, either actual or mental. Your original stop order should have been set tight, at 59¾, or at the lowest, 59½. When the stock price rises to $70 at Point 3, should you raise your stop? There are two trains of thought on this subject. People of minimum intelligence and above would say yes. Idiots would say no.

Allow me to digress a moment on this point. Let's say you make $100,000 trading stocks and, like all intelligent investors, decide to take this loot down to your bank and put it into a certificate of deposit. And let's say you made another $100,000 working nights as a ditch digger, putting this money into another certificate of deposit. Now tragedy strikes. For the third time this year, you lose your prepaid bus pass. To complicate matters, you never learned how to ride a bike. Just when you figure you are ripe for a change of luck, sure enough your Uncle Earl dies. Aunt Myrtle, who can't drive, wants to sell you Earl's 1980 Olds Cutlass. It is in mint condition with less than 40,000 below the speed limit miles on it. In fact, they still haven't ripped the protective plastic off the rear seat. On top of that, you are sure you can knock something off Aunt Myrtle's $1,000 asking price.

Of course, this is all too good to believe. You know there has to be a catch somewhere. Sure enough, there is, and in the usual place, your friendly bank. The certificate of deposit containing the money you earned breaking your back digging ditches came due today, but the certificate containing the easy loot you made trading stocks doesn't come due for another month. To complicate matters, the place you buy your bus passes closes in 10 minutes. What should you do?

As far as I'm concerned, you have two options, and not the ones you think you have. In fact, they are both far more distasteful. You can either see a psychiatrist or, worse yet, take an economics course. The common object of both of these options would be to get it through your thick skull that there is no damn difference in value between a dollar earned digging ditches and a dollar earned trading stocks—a dollar earned strip mining and one earned stripping—a dollar lost and a dollar found.

Now you are probably wondering what this all has to do with stock trading, that is, if you still remember that stock trading was the supposed subject of this book. Well it all goes back to four paragraphs ago when you bought long at $60 with a stop order at 59¾. The question then, when the stock price went up to $70, was if you should move up your stop order. The answer is, "Damn right, you should!" The logic behind this answer is that there is absolutely no difference in value between a $10 profit not yet taken and a $10 bill in your wallet. You protect one to the same degree you protect the other. If you can't get this principle through your skull, trading stocks is not for you.

Your next stop order does not, and likely should not, have to be set at ¼ below market value. You don't want to get knocked off the back of a hot stock because some little old lady in Iowa gets conned into selling her stocks to pay for a new roof she does not need in the first place. Feel free to set your new stop order around $69. At Point 6, where share price has gone up to $80, and you have made a 33⅓ percent paper profit of $20, you can be even more reckless and reset it at $78. Just remember that a dollar paper profit has the exact same value to you as a dollar in your pocket. And be thankful that Uncle Sam cannot say the same thing.

Before we leave Figure 2.5, a word of caution. When riding a stock through a euphoric rise like that between Points 7 and 10, you shouldn't be thinking about what you are going to do with your profits, I don't care how mint Uncle Earl's Cutlass may be. You should be updating your exit strategy, thinking about when and where to take those profits. Keep in mind that things are happening quicker than they were a few points down that chart. If you aren't moving up your stop order a lot faster now, then you're not moving it fast enough.

Remember, Figure 2.5, like our model previously, is merely a tool to teach you about price behavior. Price behavior is basically an interaction between supply and demand. A chart is a visual representation of this interaction. Though supply and demand seem to strive to stay in balance, they don't always succeed. As a stock trader, it will certainly pay you to know ahead of time when a market will go out of balance. Even more important, it will often cost you when you don't. Learning how to know is not an event such as turning on a light. It is a continuous learning process that builds on current knowledge.

chapter 3

indicators

how to stalk a trend

The Kinematic Model discussed in Chapter 2 is a far from per-fect indicator of a stock's future. I would not recommend any-one bet the family farm on it, if the family farm still exists by the time this book is published. However, this model is not merely a learning tool, it is an applicable tool designed to be applied with other tools by people who have acquired the knowledge and refined the discipline necessary to effectively use such tools.

The Kinematic Model cannot guarantee the future behav-ior of a particular stock. No indicator or combination of indica-tors can. Still, if you discover parallels between this model and the behavior of a stock, and these parallels encompass buy or sell signals, this should raise your interest in taking a position in the stock. However, before you do, you must first look at the stock again through the filters of every other relevant indica-tor. These indicators can reflect the market as a whole or spe-cific segments of it. Some enable you to determine the trend and trade with it. Other indicators are predictors derived from and to be applied to a particular stock. Over the years I've come across enough indicators to threaten my own sanity, not to mention questioning the sanity of their authors and the peo-ple who waste their time using them. If you want a theoretical explanation on how the phases of the moon affect stock prices, you bought the wrong book. This chapter covers only those in-dicators I judge most worthwhile, giving a brief description of them and their proper use.

There are three types of indicators: sentiment, flow-of-funds, and market structure indicators. The day trader is primarily concerned with market structure indicators, but he must also be cognizant of sentiment and flow-of-funds indicators.

Sentiment indicators deal with psychology. They monitor groups of people—some usually right about the market and some usually wrong—and draw conclusions based on the behavior of these groups. The put/call ratio is a sentiment indicator. When there is a high ratio of puts to calls, mass sentiment is predicting that the market is heading down. However, mass sentiment is usually wrong. Therefore, a high put/call ratio is actually indicating an imminent rise in the market. By the way, the put/call ratio *should not* be applied on an individual basis. Even if you consider yourself snake-bit, mass sentiment incarnate, don't bother doing exactly the opposite of what you think you should be doing. Been tried. Don't work. Besides, it will make you dizzy just trying to figure out what is the opposite and who is you. *Technical Trading Online* is written for technical traders prepared to get slightly more technical than this.

Odd lot short sales—sales of less than one hundred shares—are another sentiment indicator. Such sales are the province of the small player—the least professional, the least informed, the least successful trader. So here is another case where the informed trader bets against the amateur.

Conversely, floor specialist short sales are a signal to get onboard. Floor specialists tend to be right. If you can figure out what they are doing, you would be wise to follow suit.

Mutual funds are a driving force in the market. However, when they are fully invested, they have to cut down on their driving. These rest stops often help cause and/or coincide with the topping out of the market. This is not the time for the stock trader to jump in long.

Flow of funds indicators include mutual funds cash, hedge funds cash, insurance company cash, bank customer's cash, and brokerage customer's free balances. Is this cash available or is it fully invested and margined out? Is there fuel to feed the fire of a rising market? Also, be aware that a rise in interest rates can divert available funds from stocks to bonds.

Market structure indicators involve, among other things, price trends, cycles, volume, and their interrelationships. The following are the market structure indicators and techniques I find most valuable.

S&P cash to futures relationship

To make this relationship easier to understand, we will focus on gold for a moment. If you could buy gold in the cash market for $300 and you could sell it three months from now for $400, would you be willing to do so? I certainly hope so. I myself would be more than willing. What if the market price of gold went up to $310 and the futures price went down to $390, would you still be willing to take this position? I certainly would. If you have a better way to make money, I should be reading your book. In fact, I wouldn't be too proud to jump at a substantially smaller profit. Neither would your average gold trader. Let's take a look at how they would react.

If the price of gold in the cash market is $300 and the futures price is $400, you can buy the gold immediately and contract to sell it in three months for $400. This is a $100 or 33 percent profit in just three months. Forgive me for showing off my math skills, but that results in an annual profit of 132 percent, ignoring lost interest and other costs. Traders will certainly increase buying pressure in the cash market. This increase in demand will raise the current price. Remember, buying stems not from any intention to hoard the gold, but rather to contract to sell it in the future. Therefore, an increase in current demand entails an increase in future supply. This increase in supply will decrease the price of gold futures. In case your mouth is watering at the thought of the next $100 gap between gold cash to futures, I should warn you not to wait around for it. This example has been a more than slight exaggeration. The same market pressures that would narrow such an end-of-the-rainbow gap would also prevent one in the first place.

Now let's get back to the stock market. The Standard & Poor's 500 Index represents 500 specific stocks taken as a whole. You can buy and sell futures contracts based on it. Hypothetically, let us say that the S&P 500 is at 1000. You may think of this 1000 as meaning the basket of stocks this index is based on is selling for $1000. Again hypothetically, let us say the futures contract on this basket is selling at $1100. Obviously, there is optimism about the future prospects of the stock market, and it has driven up the futures price. The result is a locked-in profit—an *arbitrage*—if someone buys the stocks encompassed by the S&P 500 and also sells a futures contract on them. These conditions will entice traders, some of them very big players, into doing just that.

The buying pressure means increased demand that will increase the cash price of these stocks. The increased supply and selling pressure means a decrease in the futures price. As in the previous gold example, the gap between the two prices will narrow. Therefore, in general, when cash price is lower than futures price by a significant margin over the interest that could have been earned and other costs, conditions are favorable for buying stock. In part as a self-fulfilling prophecy, buying pressure by itself will help raise the stock price, which was the expectation that made conditions for buying favorable in the first place. The relationship between the cash market and the futures market is extremely important in determining the trend of the market.

Of course determining the trend means determining whether people are going to buy stock and sell futures causing an uptrend, or do the opposite causing a downtrend. So how do we calculate exactly which is a better buy—stock or futures? We don't. This is already calculated for us and is a readily available statistic called *Fair Value.*

Fair Value takes into account the fact that $100 in your possession today is worth more than a guaranteed $100 three months from now. To understand this, you have to ignore, however comforting it may be, the fact that in three months you will have a guaranteed credit of $100. Admittedly, not every stock trader can feel so secure. On the other hand, you may starve to death in the meantime. Also, if you had the $100 today, you could probably live off all the interest and a few friends, and still have the $100 principal in three months. Whether you would still have the friends is another question. Of course, if you would get serious about finishing this book, you could trade stocks with the $100 and turn it into a fortune. I assure you, nothing facilitates new friendships better than a large fortune.

It is also important that you understand how the terms bullish and bearish are applied to the cash-to-futures relationship. Let us assume the S&P Cash Market (SPX) closes strong at 1280, and the S&P Futures Market (SP/mg) closes at 1289. The next morning you come in and CNBC is saying that S&P Futures are up 1.0 and really bullish. You sit there wondering how up 1.0 can be really bullish. Well CNBC is taking into account that the SP/mg was already 9.0 over cash, now it is 10.0 over.

The Fair Value we are interested in refers to a standard three-month contract, one of four that run consecutively throughout the year. Specifically, it refers to the current one, that which is closest to coming due. It is important to keep this in mind because as the term of the contract expires, the time of payment draws closer, and therefore the Fair Value of the contract should move toward the sum of the actual payment to be made.

Remember, Fair Value is not a figure you have to compute. One of the easier ways to find it is by tuning in to CNBC. Their talking heads cannot go more than a few minutes without mentioning it. Market pressures tend to push market values in the direction of Fair Value. Any substantial difference between the two that is caused by market inefficiencies will bring on a stampede of arbitragers to scarf up the locked-in profits thus made available. However, the effect of all the individual arbitragers is dwarfed by that of automatic computer programs. When these pachyderms stampede, all you itty bitty traders want to be running in the right direction—and running fast.

For example, let us assume CNBC says, "Fair Value is 4.76 over." This means that the price of the current S&P Futures contract should be 4.76 more than the current S&P 500 Index (4.76 over cash). If it is close, relationships are rational and should be fairly stable. Now CNBC also provides us with two figures that make the Fair Value figure even more valuable to you. In this case, CNBC tells us that the computer buy programs will kick in at 7.24 over cash and the sell programs at 2.48 over cash. Both of these figures are positive, and they bracket the Fair Value of 4.76. If you see cash approaching either of these brackets, you better find yourself an elephant to ride or get the hell out of the jungle. Take advantage of my vast experience in the bush when I say that it is considerably easier to jump up on an elephant before it starts to stampede. If you insist on waiting, you better at least be running in the same direction.

advances versus declines

The relationship between all 3000 advancing and declining issues on the New York Stock Exchange is a statistic readily
available throughout the day. If there is a better indicator of
the trend of the market as a whole, I haven't found it. The chart
below represents this relationship, though the swings de-
scribed have been exaggerated for purposes of illustration:

	Advancing Issues	Declining	Unchanged
10:00 A.M.	500	2000	500
12:00 P.M.	900	1500	600
2:00 P.M.	2000	500	500
3:55 P.M.	1250	1250	500

What is the trend at 10:00 A.M.? Obviously, it is down, and
you can bet that at least a few of those declining issues would
and should be advancing except for the mood of the market as a
whole. So what about Organic Junk Foods, Inc., that stock you
have been watching for weeks? You almost bought it yesterday.
This morning you heard some additional favorable information
about it. An upturn is looking even more likely. Something tells
you the hell with the trend, "Buy now!" Well that something sure
isn't our Rule 3. So what should you do? Plain and simple, you
should wait for a reversal of trend in the market as a whole. If
you are a day trader, you should also start looking for a stock to
sell short. The best place to look is in a group of stocks (banks,
oil and gas, and so on) that is even weaker than the market as a
whole. The best stock to sell short in that group should be one
of the weakest. Weak stocks are more likely to move with the
downtrend, getting even weaker.

What is the trend at 2:00 P.M.? Before we get into that,
let's hope that by now our day trader has covered that stock

he or she sold short at 10:00 A.M. And if Organic Junk Food, Inc. was still looking strong a few hours ago, let's hope he or she went ahead and bought it. Back to 2:00 P.M.. What's the trend? I'll give you a hint. The 12:00 P.M. figures were a good indication that the 10:00 A.M. downtrend was reversing. The trend at 2:00 P.M. is up. You day traders should get busy and find a stock to go long. Again, the best place to look is in a stock group even stronger than the market as a whole. Strong stocks are more likely to move with the uptrend, getting even stronger. And the best stock should be one of the strongest in the group.

Now let's check out 3:55 P.M.. Again the question is, "What is the trend?" The answer is, "What trend?" If you really insist on buying something now, I would suggest a cold beer on your way home. By the way, if you think the preceding chart means that you should go in every day and sell short at 10:00 A.M. and buy long at 2:00 P.M., then perhaps in your case this book is not the ideal tool with which to make your fortune. You might try a shovel or a broom instead.

the trader's index

The Trader's Index, also called the Arms Index, is named after its inventor, Richard Arms:

$$\frac{\text{Advancing issues}/\text{Declining issues}}{\text{Advancing volume}/\text{Declining volume}} = N$$

If N is >1, for example 1.90, the market is bearish. If N is < 1, for example 0.48, the market is bullish. The value of N is of interest, but of greater interest are the changes in N.

Let's say N was 0.50, and you went long. N moves to 0.55 and then to 0.60. N is becoming less bullish, moving closer to

1.0. If and when it crosses 1.0, the market trend will have reversed, switching from bullish to bearish. The Trader's Index is telling you to sell or be ready to sell.

Or let's say N was 1.50 and you sold short. N rises to 1.60, then 1.90. The Trader's Index is moving away from 1.0, indicating a strengthening downtrend, getting more bearish. It is telling you to hold your short position.

Remember, any time the Trader's Index moves significantly toward 1.0, the market trend is reversing. If your position is based on the existing trend, especially you day traders, you better think hard and fast about abandoning it.

comparative relative strength

Comparative relative strength refers to a stock's performance relative to a market indicator. The question it should answer is whether a stock is weaker or stronger than the market as a whole. There are numerous indexes you can use to measure the market's strength such as the S&P 500 Index, S&P Futures Index, the Dow Jones Index, and so on. If, for instance, the S&P 500 Index is rising as in Figure 3.1a, and a stock price is moving

figure 3.1   relative strength

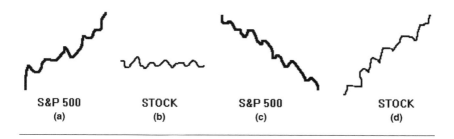

S&P 500   STOCK   S&P 500   STOCK
  (a)   (b)   (c)   (d)

sideways as in Figure 3.1b, what signal should you watch for? First of all, we can see that the stock is weak relative to the market. At the first sign of a downturn in the S&P 500 Index, you should seriously consider selling the stock short unless there is a compelling reason why the mood of the overall market will not effect this stock's price negatively. Likewise, if the S&P 500 is declining as in Figure 3.1c, and the stock's price, as in Figure 3.1d, is rising steadily despite this, you should seriously consider buying long at the first signs of an upturn. Comparative relative strength is one of the most reliable stock market tools. It is of great value to all traders, from day to swing to position.

oscillators

To make money trading stocks, and I'm of course talking about untold millions, all you really have to know are two things: when to buy and when to sell. I apologize for not letting the cat out of the bag sooner, but at least I didn't wait until the last sentence of the last chapter to give this secret away. Another thing I can now give away is the unfortunate fact that this book can't tell you when to buy or when to sell. It can only teach you how to figure this out for yourself.

Amazingly, an oscillator, a mere two-dimensional chart, can predict trend reversals, thereby telling you when to buy and sell. Not so amazingly, it can often tell you wrong.

This type of prediction when proven true can be more than helpful, it can be valuable. Therefore, we try to gauge such predictions with other indicators, such as the Kinematic Model. If the application of our model indicates you should sell a stock short, and an oscillator indicates this stock is overbought, you should be able to act with more conviction than if going by our model alone. Take a look at Figure 3.2. Only the solid line concerns us now. At Point 3, the stock is considered overbought because this line lies between Lines *A* and *B*. This indicates a correction in the offing—too much buying has taken place and selling is about to take over. At Point 5, the solid line is between Lines *D* and *E*, indicating that the stock is oversold—too much selling has taken place. This means a recovery is probably on the way, with an increase in demand and price in the near future. Again, an oversold stock should be in line for a price rise, an overbought one should be in line for a price decline.

figure 3.2   oscillator

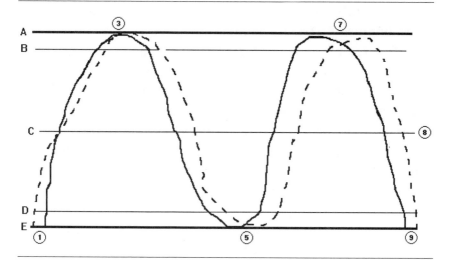

Some oscillators give their indication—their buy or sell signal—by crossing a zero line, Line *C,* as occurs at Point 8. Other oscillators, such as a stochastic, consist of two lines—a fast solid one and a slow dotted one. In this case, the fast one, referred to as percentage *K,* is the result of a complicated mathematical formula that takes into consideration momentum, rate of change, and range comparisons. The dotted second line, the percentage *D* line, is a moving average of the percentage *K* line, and therefore moves more slowly. A stochastic gives its buy or sell signals when percentage *K,* the solid line, crosses percentage *D,* the dotted line. Crossover that occurs in the overbought area between Lines *A* and *B,* such as Point 3, is a sell signal. Crossover that occurs in the oversold area between Lines *D* and *E,* such as at Point 5, is a buy signal.

The RSI is another oscillator. Though a relative strength indicator, it is very different from comparative relative strength. The RSI measures a stock's relative strength compared to itself as opposed to an index. It is derived from a complicated formula that takes into consideration not only a stock's selling price, but also its trading volume and other factors.

To use this oscillator, you have no more need to know how it is computed, than you have a need to know how a watch works in order to tell time. I have to mention that I am sparing you a detailed explanation despite the fact that doing so would not only allow me to pad this book by another ten pages, but also despite the additional fact that the last time I explained how the RSI is computed, about half way through, for at least a good two seconds, I could have sworn I actually understood it myself.

To use the RSI, you must keep in mind that it usually tops above 70 and bottoms below 30, doing so before the stock price reverses trend. However, the real value of this indicator is as a warning system. For example, take a look at Figure 3.3. Notice that while the stock is making a new high, the RSI is already on its way down. This divergence is clearly predicting a reversal of trend in the near future.

There are numerous other oscillators we could discuss. However, we won't. In my experience, the stochastic and the RSI are far and away the most helpful, especially when used in conjunction with each other. The MACD oscillator (moving average convergence divergence) too often trails price behavior. Despite this unfortunate fact, it remains quite popular. Perhaps people feel that hindsight's infallibility somehow makes up for its lack of timeliness. It is a pity that there is no security

figure 3.3 RSI

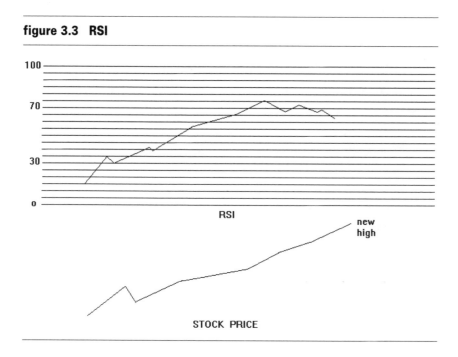

pegged to the MACD of a basket of stock. We could all get rich using the price of this basket to predict the MACD.

In the meantime, keep in mind that there are three basic buy or sell signals an oscillator can give you:

1. When it enters or crosses over in an overbought area,
2. When it enters or crosses over in an oversold area, and
3. When it crosses a zero line.

ACPS

The ACPS is the average cents per share that stocks on the New York Stock Exchange are up or down. For example, an ACPS of +50 means that the average stock share is up fifty cents. An ACPS of –50 means the average share is down fifty cents.

This indicator's significance as a measure of the market's strength is not so much in the number itself, but rather in its direction and rate of change. For example, if a 10:00 A.M. ACPS of +50 declines to +35 by 10:15 A.M., the inference would be a weakening market.

The ACPS is especially incisive when used in conjunction with advance/decline figures. Let us say that at 11:00 A.M. the advance/decline is 1805 up/590 down, while the ACPS is +50. Then at 11:15 A.M. we have an advance/decline of 1810 up/580 down. Yet the ACPS has dropped to +30. Though the advance/decline is indicating a strengthening market, the ACPS indicates a weakening one. In this case, the ACPS is the more convincing indicator. A good guess as to what is behind these figures is that the market is experiencing some profit taking. Supply is coming in and stock prices are weakening as traders nail down some profits.

price and volume

Price tells us what is happening. Volume tells us how it is happening. Let's say you have a stock with an average daily trading volume of about one million shares and a normal price fluctuation of about a point. One day it trades two million shares and goes up four points. Any day trader who does not find this action interesting should be checked for a pulse. A train appears to be leaving the station and a shot of adrenaline in his or her bloodstream should be yelling, "Jump aboard!" Well if you think adrenaline levels are the key to successful day trading, you might as well throw this book away because it sure won't save your balance sheet. Any stock trader in the habit of jumping aboard trains without first trying to figure out where they are headed will eventually end up as blood on the tracks.

The question is, "How do you keep your emotions in check to analyze a fast-moving situation such as this with a stone-cold eye?" The answer is, "Through rote." Whenever you are enticed by the movement of a stock, force yourself to examine it through the very same frame of reference—that of supply and demand. Ask yourself the same, exact, seven-word question: What is happening with supply and demand? I cannot guarantee that you will come up with an answer, but merely by asking the question, I can guarantee a large, sudden drop in your adrenaline level.

Getting back to our example, the stock's volume not only jumped, it doubled from one million to two million. Share price also jumped, four points, as opposed to a daily average movement of a single point. I hope you remember the question we now force ourselves to ask. If not, check back six sentences. Supply is obviously still there, but the demand has outstripped it. Let us assume that out of the two million share volume, 1,800,000 came in as buy orders and 200,000 came in as sell orders.

Now the next day volume stayed just as high, two million shares. Yet the stock price only went up a quarter. What does this tell us about supply and demand? It tells us that supply and demand are more or less in balance. So now we know not only what is happening, we know how it is happening.

In addition to knowing what is happening and how it is happening, it is important to know *where* it is happening. Is it in an accumulation phase, a distribution phase, an uptrend, or a downtrend? Are price/volume relationships giving strong indications as to future action. For example, in an uptrend when you see volume drop on a reaction and rise again on a rally, this indicates a continuation of the uptrend. Therefore, a long position is called for. Conversely, in a downtrend, if volume drops in a rally and rises again during the following price decline, this indicates a continuation of the downtrend, time for the trader to be selling short.

Let us look at some less obvious scenarios. Assume on a particular day a stock rises four points on a volume of 100,000 shares. Average daily volume had been one million shares. If we want to know where the stock is going to go from here, we better find out exactly where "here" is. This suspicious breaking of resistance on low volume tends to indicate the end of a distribution phase and a Shake-Up-Fake-Out-Before-the-Breakdown. Such analysis may not supply us with enough conviction to sell short, but it is fair warning against going long.

Alternately, let us say a high volume of supply has been coming in to meet demand, creating a ceiling the stock price cannot surpass. It is very likely that this resistance is taking place at the end of a distribution trading range. As it begins to seem less and less likely that the stock price will break through the resistance line, demand will more than likely decrease, taking the stock price with it into a markdown phase. Looking at the same phenomenon from a different angle, we can say that high volume at the top of a distribution range, with a narrow price spread, tells us that supply and demand are in equilibrium. If demand falls, so will price.

Conversely, if we get high volume and a very narrow price spread just off the support line of an accumulation phase, what does this tell us? It tells us that increased demand is sucking up supply, which in turn means we should expect a markup phase imminently.

As regards both uptrends and downtrends, increasing volume in the direction of the trend and decreasing volume on reactions indicate a continuation of these trends. The opposite indicates a possible imminent reversal of trend. When facing the latter, the aware trader, especially the day trader, should not only consider abandoning his position, but also possibly reversing it.

crossovers

Monitoring crossovers is a very popular technique of some very successful traders, especially day traders. The superior quote screens provided by some online information services can be set to show advancing issues in green and declining issues in red. The individual quotes can also be arranged in groups, which usually means by industry. Let us say you are studying the pharmaceutical group and see mostly red. This tells you that the pharmaceutical group is bearish. If on another day it is mostly green, this means the group is bullish.

Assume a particular stock opens at 80 and goes down two points. There are now a lot of buyers who have positioned wrong at 80 and want out. If the stock rises back up to 80, many of these buyers will bail. This means they will add to supply, perhaps sending the stock back down to 78, and up and down again in a trading range. Each time the price rises back to 80, the added supply will keep it from rising over 80. This makes 80 a point of resistance. However, eventually, if this movement continues, all the people who want to bail out and break even for the day at 80 will get the chance to do so. Now the stock may go up to 80⅛, crossing over from a declining to an advancing issue, and from red to green.

That change in color is the eye-catching shattering of a psychological barrier, especially to the day trader. That ⅛ point change in color is very often enough to get his butt off the bench and onto the field, thus giving the stock a real boost. Here the day trader was, looking for, praying for a stock with momentum, when a dinky ⅛ point of change which most likely would have been ignored if it had not entailed a change in color from red to green, sets off this huge adrenaline rush in him and all his day trading friends, a rush strong enough to turn an imagined ⅛ point of momentum into some bona fide momentum, thus giving the stock a healthy and profitable boost. Nowhere is prophecy as potentially self-fulfilling as in the stock market, at least in the short run.

Prophecy aside, the fact that share price has broken through a point of resistance is an additional indication that this stock, at the very least, should be watched carefully. Supply just may be exhausted. A sharp rise in price would tend to confirm this. If this stock goes on to pass its all-time high, let's say 86, it will break another point of resistance. This may cause short covering, the unleashing of pent-up demand, and the activation of automatic buy stop orders. It is no coincidence that buy stops are often clustered above resistance points. Many traders use these orders to enter long positions on significant signs of strength. Obviously, this activation, along with short covering and the unleashing of pent-up demand should in concert cause an additional jump in price.

quick quotes

GM	L 86¼	Chg +3	B 86⅛	A 86⅝	S 10 x 8	V 2,183,300
O 85	H 86¼	Lo 84½	AH 87¼	AL 47⅛	LTV 100	
N 1:59	C 83¼	EPS 3.93	PER 21.95	DIV 2.00	Y 2.32	EX 11/9/98

On the first line we have the stock symbol, GM for General Motors. The last trade (L) was at 86¼. The change (Chg) is plus 3 from the previous day's close. The bid (B) is 86⅛. The asking price (A) is 86⅝. The size (S) is 1,000 shares on the bid side and 800 on the offered. The total volume traded (V) that day up to the second is 2,183,300 shares. On the second line, the opening price (O) for the day is 85. The day's high (H) is 86¼. The day's low (Lo) is 84½. The all-time high (AH) is 87¼. The all-time low (AL) is 47⅛. The last trade's volume was 100 shares. On the third line, N stands for New York Stock Exchange. The previous night's close (C) was 83¼. The earnings per share (EPS) is $3.93. The price/earnings ratio (PER) is 21.95. The dividend (DIV) it pays is $2.00. The yield right now is 2.32 percent. It went ex-dividend (EX) 11/9/98.

You can trade off a quick quote using the opening price as a support or resistance point, and using the all-time high as a resistance point.

candlesticks

We will not discuss bar charts in this book because the subject is fairly straightforward, there are myriad books that cover the subject, and it would put us all to sleep. We will discuss candlesticks, an increasingly popular charting technique, and one that I endorse wholeheartedly.

Candlesticks were developed by the Japanese about three hundred years ago to chart price activity in a way that facilitates the gauging of markets. They are every bit as useful today. Candlesticks remained a secret to the Western world until 10 years ago when Steve Nison brought them to our attention. He remains the pre-eminent round-eyed authority on candlesticks. I highly recommend his book, *Japanese Candlestick Charting Techniques* (New York Institute of Finance, Simon & Schuster, 1991, New York).

We have just examined the Quick Quote. It tells us a lot about a stock, sometimes too much. Deriving only the information we want from all the information listed can be confusing. When trading, especially day trading, the speed with which one acts can spell the difference between profit and loss. Some mental input does require thought, but much of it can be processed by reflex in a fraction of the time. In day trading particularly, information that *can* be handled reflexively *must* be handled reflexively to save time. Candlesticks offer at a glance information that must be derived from a Quick Quote, plus additional information about supply and demand.

In Figure 3.4 we have the two kinds of candlesticks, one white or hollow and one black or solid. The widest part of the candlestick is referred to as the real body. We will refer to it as the body. Usually, but not always, a line extends from the top of the body, the bottom, or both. The Japanese refer to this line as an upper or lower shadow. We shall call it the wick. The corresponding parts of both candlesticks in Figure 3.4 represent the exact same dollar values. Yet these two candlesticks represent different, in some ways opposite, market conditions.

figure 3.4   candlestick characteristics

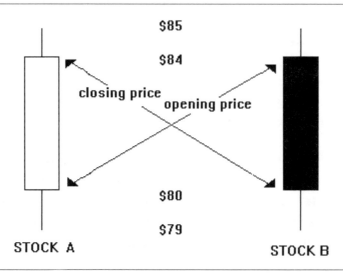

$85

$84

closing price

opening price

$80

$79

STOCK A

STOCK B

The white or hollow candlestick tells us that Stock A opened at $80, a value that corresponds to the bottom of the candlestick's body. At some time during the day, it fell to a low of $79, as represented by the lowest point of the bottom wick. Also, at some time during the day, this stock reached a high of $85, as represented by the highest point of the top wick. The top of the body, located to signify $84, represents the closing price of Stock A. Though both the day's high and low are important, the Japanese consider the opening and closing prices as even more important. Because this stock closed higher than it opened, it is represented by a bullish white or hollow candlestick.

The bearish black or solid candlestick always represents a stock that closed lower than it opened. In Figure 3.4, aside from color, the only difference between the two candlesticks is that Stock B opened at $84 and closed down, at $80.

Look how much one quick glance tells us about the stocks represented by these two candlesticks. Stock A closed up $4, while Stock B closed down $4. Their days' highs were $85, and their lows were $79. Because of the wide price range represented by these candlesticks, we can infer that demand controlled the price of Stock A, and supply controlled the price of Stock B. However, the greatest value of candlesticks is their ability to represent the movement of one particular stock at intervals ranging from minutes to years. These representations not only give quick insight into the interactions of supply and demand on the stock, they enable you to pick up the trend at a glance, often warning you about imminent reversals of trend. A trick to help you remember that a white or hollow candlestick is bullish is to remember that hollow conveys lightness or floating up. The bearish black or solid candlestick conveys solidness, heaviness, and sinking.

It is time for a quick course on what the different shapes of some candlesticks tell us. The longer the body of a candlestick, the more bullish or bearish the stock it represents. Candlesticks with very small bodies, such as that representing Stock C in Figure 3.5, portray very small price ranges for the period represented. They are referred to as spinning tops. Stock C, though bullish, is only barely so. Supply and demand are almost in balance.

The candlesticks representing Stocks D and E are referred to as *shaved topped*. Stock D closed at its high, a bullish point that adds some more bull to an already bullish stock. Stock E never once beat its opening price, a bearish point to consider.

The candlesticks representing Stocks F and G are referred to as *shaved bottomed*. Stock F never sunk below its opening price, a slightly bullish point. Stock G did manage to top its opening price. Still, it closed down at its low for the period—a bearish point.

---

figure 3.5 candlestick shapes

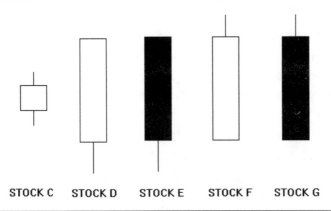

STOCK C   STOCK D   STOCK E   STOCK F   STOCK G

In Figure 3.6, the almost bodiless candlestick representing Stock H is called a *Doji*. We can see from the $4 range that there was quite a battle between demand and supply, which ended in a draw, meaning no change in share price for the day. A slight change in price still qualifies as a Doji, as does a

figure 3.6 Doji candlesticks

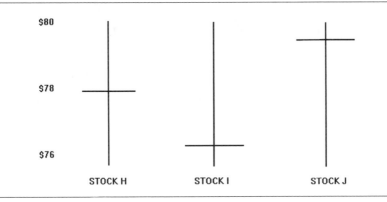

$80

$78

$76

STOCK H   STOCK I   STOCK J

candlestick which had a range that went higher or lower in one direction than in the other, as those representing Stocks I and J.

Let us take a look now at Figure 3.7 which describes the movement of one particular stock over a period of days. Only the last day is represented by an actual candlestick. This particular type of candlestick is called a *Hanging Man.* It can be black or white, but it has to occur during an uptrend. It can have a very small upper wick. The defining feature is that the lower wick must be at least twice as long as the body. If you can picture the very small upper wick as a head, and the long lower wick as legs, then you can actually picture this candlestick as a hanging man. You will soon see that it is no coincidence that its name has an ominous sound.

What does the candlestick in Figure 3.7a tell us? First of all, it is black or solid, which means the stock closed down. It also gapped open and barely beat its opening price. Share price took a free fall, but did make somewhat of a recovery. If I had a position long on this stock, I would be worried. If the body were white instead of black, I would be only slightly less

figure 3.7   the Hammer and Hanging Man candlesticks

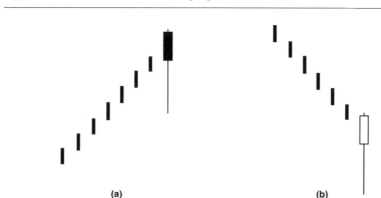

(a)   (b)

worried. The prolonged upturn in price seems to be losing momentum and a reversal of trend could be in the offing.

Now take a look at Figure 3.7b. Here we have a prolonged downtrend. The bullish candlestick at the bottom, though shaped like a Hanging Man, is called a *Hammer*. It tells us a serious price drop ended in a recovery, and the stock closed up. This looks like another reversal of trend, but in the opposite direction. If the candlestick had been black, this would have made it only slightly less bullish.

Another signal of reversal is an *Engulfing Pattern*. First let us examine one at the end of an uptrend, as in Figure 3.8a. The second to last candlestick is bullish and gives no sign of a reversal. The big, black, bearish Engulfing Pattern that follows and overshadows it signals a possible reversal of trend. Figure 3.8b. is the negative image, this time telling you to go long. The Engulfing Pattern must be the opposite color of the preceding candlestick.

Two of the strongest reversal patterns are the *Doji Morning* and *Evening Stars*. The Doji Morning Star appears during a downtrend as depicted in Figure 3.9a. It gaps open and closes

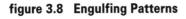

figure 3.8   Engulfing Patterns

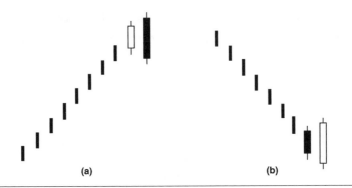

(a)   (b)

---

figure 3.9 Doji Morning and Evening Stars

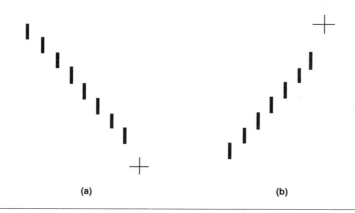

(a)   (b)

---

at or very near the same price. Its opposite, Figure 3.9b, is the Doji Evening Star.

Candlesticks can give extraordinary insight into market behavior, and they can do so at a glance. There are many other illuminating types we have not discussed. Try to apply the ones we have discussed. If you find them helpful, you will find a look at Mr. Nison's book even more so.

the Dow Theory

Although the Dow Theory is somewhat overrated and out-dated, a day trader should be acquainted with it. Dow Jones' three major averages are Industrials, Transports, and Utilities. The Industrials includes thirty stocks, the Transports fifteen, and the Utilities twelve. These averages originated back in the 1920s, but they have been updated, Microsoft being the most recent addition. However, these updates still fail to include many of the Internet stocks that are such driving forces in today's market. Additionally, these indexes are comprised of a

---

relatively very small number of stocks. Therefore, the S&P 500 and the New York Stock Exchange Composite are far better indicators of the market as a whole. Still, the Dow Jones Averages do retain quite a bit of credence.

The Utility Average reflects interest rates. The lower the rates, the more money business can borrow for expansion and other needs. If business is going well, it is manufacturing and selling goods. Collaterally, earnings are healthy and so are stock prices. However, just because industry is operating at full tilt, it does not necessarily follow that the goods produced are being shipped. They could merely be expanding inventory. So the health of the industrial sector must also be reflected in the health of the transportation sector.

Remember, the main importance of the Utility Average is as an indicator of the trend in interest rates. If the Dow Jones Utility Average is rising, this indicates that interest rates are going down. Low interest rates allow for the expansion of business, sending the Industrial Average higher. Low interest rates also encourage capital to flow into the stock market as opposed to the bond market, thus protecting and even increasing stock prices. More goods shipped by industry raises the Transport Average. A rise in all three averages creates among traders confidence in the economy as a whole. However, when there is a divergence, and either or both Transports and Utilities are down, traders become wary no matter how high and fast the Industrial Average is rising.

On Balance Volume

These days, when everyone has access to a computer, On Balance Volume (OBV) has been somewhat supplanted by other indicators. There are a number of theoreticians' formulas for OBV, but the most popular is probably Joe Granville's. This indicator is a running total. When a stock's price goes up, its volume is added to the total. When it goes down, the volume is subtracted. For example:

Day	Price	Change	Volume	On Balance Volume
Monday	$100	+1	100,000	+100,000
Tuesday	100¼	+¼	200,000	+300,000
Wednesday	100½	+¼	500,000	+800,000
Thursday	100¼	−¼	200,000	+600,000

You use these figures as an indication as to whether a stock is under accumulation or distribution. Over time, OBV figures will give you a line. If this line trends upward, it is indicating that this particular stock is under accumulation. If it trends downward, the indication is that the stock is in a distribution phase. Make sure you check other indicators for confirmation.

OBV is most useful to the position trader. Though of little help in timing the taking of a position, it weighs in nicely on the advisability of taking that position in the first place. A stock's past and current price movement may be encouraging, but OBV offers valuable input as to whether this movement is likely to continue.

chapter 4

continuation and reversal signals for trends

**trends: oh, when will they start?
oh, when will they end?**

In our model, the accumulation and distribution phases look like those in Figure 4.1a. In the real world, it may look more like Figure 4.1b. How can you be sure Figure 4.1b is an accumulation or distribution phase? You can't, but with experience you will learn to judge with enough confidence to act with the conviction necessary to be a successful stock trader.

reversal signals

By definition, the successful trader has to be able to spot a trend. Obviously, the sooner he can do so, the sooner he can take a position and the more points he can get out of one. More important, if he has already taken a position, the sooner he can spot a reversal of trend, the sooner he can abandon this position, and the more likely he can walk away solvent.

Let us assume the market is down, and you are a day trader looking through five-minute charts for a stock to short. Contrary Conglomerations, Inc. (Figure 4.2a), catches your eye. You start observing at Point 4, and no way does this look like a good bet to sell short. Still, the way Contrary Conglomerations,

---

figure 4.1 accumulation and distribution phases

(a)   (b)

---

figure 4.2   five-minute versus daily charts

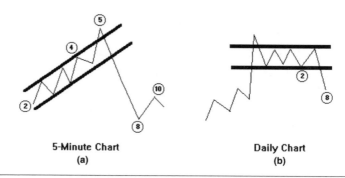

5-Minute Chart
(a)

Daily Chart
(b)

Inc., is bucking the market trend impresses you enough to keep watching it.

Well, if you like action, this stock proves worth watching. The drop in altitude from Point 5 to Point 8 makes you glad your breakfast is fully digested and your lunch isn't for another hour. To say the least, this stock has broken its support line. If it isn't headed down in an atypically violent reversal, it certainly isn't going up. Contrary Conglomerations, Inc., looks to have been (and still looks like) a good stock to sell short after all. Let us do something now that you should have done right away—check the daily charts.

What a surprise. Figure 4.2a fits neatly between Points 2 and 8 of Figure 4.2b. This big picture shows us that our apparent uptrend was merely part of—and likely the end of—our old friend the distribution phase.

If this analysis seems a little too pat, let's get closer to the real world and assume that the daily chart showed us nothing, or at least nothing we could figure out. So what happened to our stock? Who knows—legal problems, bad news,

plain bad management? Does that mean we give up day trading? Not likely. Does that mean we lose interest in Contrary
Conglomerations, Inc.? No chance. You want to go short. But
do you want to go short now or hold off a bit. Typically, it took
you so long to decide that you in fact did hold off a bit. It is just
as well, because our stock has now rallied to Point 10 on Figure 4.2a. A moment later it starts down again. Is this the time
to sell short?

Well, this is not necessarily the time to sell short, but it is
certainly the time to look for confirmation. You could try com-
paring our graph to the S&P Wave, as in Figure 4.3a. This looks
like confirmation to me. I would advise taking a look at some
other indicators, but I would do it fast. This could be a ride you
don't want to miss.

Let's take a look at the opposite occurrence, a violent reversal of a downtrend as in Figure 4.3b. That break in resistance

figure 4.3   confirmation of trends

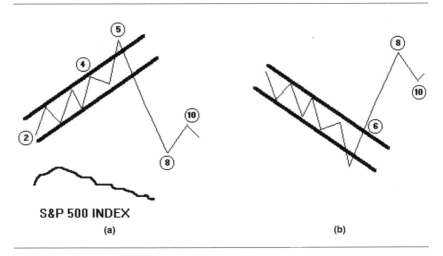

S&P 500 INDEX

(a)   (b)

at Point 6 looks like a clear buy signal. It is time for a quick search of other indicators for some confirmation. One thing you should look for is high volume between Points 6 and 8. Conversely, low volume between Points 8 and 10 tends to further confirm a temporary reaction to a reversal of trend. When this stock starts back up again, you just may want to be on it.

There are a number of signals that indicate a probable reversal of trend. Before we go on, allow me to point out that there exists a shade difference in meaning between the phrase "indicate a probable" and the phrase "guarantee a definite." Enough said? I hope so.

The most famous reversal signal is the Head and Shoulders (Figure 4.4a). If you think the high is too pointed to resemble a head, then you are one of those lucky people who hasn't had much contact with bureaucrats. The horizontal support line is sometimes referred to as the "neck." The lines below the price graph represent volume. Now Point 9 is an important test of resistance, one that failed by a large margin. This means an even

figure 4.4   reversal of trend signals

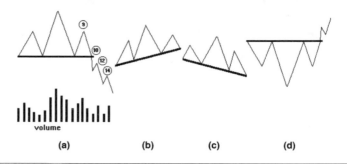

more important test is the next one, that of support at Point 10. If share price breaks the neck here, and if concurrently volume is high, then selling short looks like a very good bet. Further confirmation of a downtrend would be low volume during the short rallies that precede subsequent downward movement. This is exactly what we see in Figure 4.4a. The places to sell short are as close as possible to the break low (Point 10) and just after the peaks of the rallies that follow (Points 12 and 14, and so on).

Of course in the real world, a place many expert theorists have never had the displeasure of visiting, the neck line may slant up as in Figure 4.4b or down as in Figure 4.4c. The Head And Shoulders can also stand on its head, as in Figure 4.4d. Upside down, this graph represents the reversal of a downtrend. We would then contemplate buying long instead of selling short. All we established about buying signals and volume still holds true, only in reverse.

Another reversal signal is the *Double Top* (Figure 4.5a). The most interesting thing about this event is the psychology behind it. The Double Top is not merely an example of, it is proof positive of the memory of traders. On the ride up from Point 2 to Point 5, your average trader is wondering all the way,

figure 4.5   the Double Top and the Double Bottom

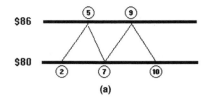

(a)

(b)

"Why should I sell now and forego additional profits?" On the ride down from Point 5 to Point 7, he is wondering, "Why the hell didn't I sell at $86? Why? Why!?" On the ride back up between Points 7 and 9, he crosses his fingers and says to himself all the way up, "If only it hits $86 again, I'll sell in an instant." Rest assured he has plenty of company. When they all try to unload at Point 9, share price drops back down to $80.

Now you are probably asking yourself, "If stock traders have such good memories, how come so many are so busy making the same old mistakes, they have barely enough time to make new mistakes?" I have a hunch much of the blame lies with the two little traits—egotism and stubbornness—with a healthy pinch of stupidity mixed in. However, you should probably be asking this question of a psychologist.

Our next reversal signal, Figure 4.5b, is the *Double Bottom*. Congratulations if you spot some similarities to the Double Top. Suffice to say, the Double Bottom works just like the Double Top, except, if you"ll pardon the technical jargon, upside down and opposite.

The *Triple Top* (Figure 4.6a) is merely a Double Top, only more so, 50 percent more so to be exact. It could also be called

figure 4.6   the Triple Bottom

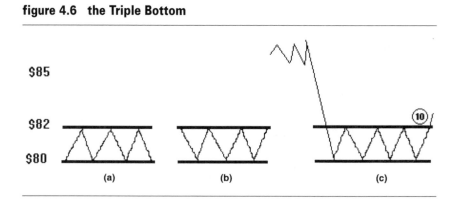

a trading range, and of course everything we have learned about these ranges can be applied to it. So as not to insult your intelligence, I will leave you to figure out the implications of a Triple Bottom (Figure 4.6b). You might start with trying to find the only difference between Figures 4.6a and 4.6b. Take all the time you need.

If by now you have not found the difference between Figures 4.6a and 4.6b, I doubt you are going to. Figure 4.6c is actually a quadruple bottom, which for our purposes is the same thing as both a Triple Bottom and a plain old trading range. Let's assume you came upon this graph while checking the five-minute charts around 2:30 P.M. The stock started out by dropping five points at the beginning of the day. Around 11:00 A.M. it settled down into a two point trading range. Then a few minutes ago, it broke the resistance line at Point 10. This is an obvious buy signal, and we should start checking, and checking fast, some other indicators for confirmation. Experience, if you possess it, will tell you something else. When a move like this happens around 2:30 P.M., there is a good chance a lot of traders are second guessing the five-point drop from yesterday's close. Before the final bell, this stock is likely to make up at least some of those five points it lost. A strategically placed buy stop, as an entry strategy, will grab a few of them for you. If it does, and if subsequently you have similar success on other days, these pleasant experiences will become ingrained in your memory. You will start paying attention, not only to what is happening and how it is happening, but also *when* in the trading day it is happening. Such awareness cannot help but make you a better, and therefore more profitable, trader.

Another often encountered denizen of the five-minute charts is a reversal signal called the *Descending Triangle* (Figure 4.7a). Here we have a stock that has been in an uptrend. It makes a peak at Point 5, then a lower peak at Point 7, and an

figure 4.7   Descending and Ascending Triangles

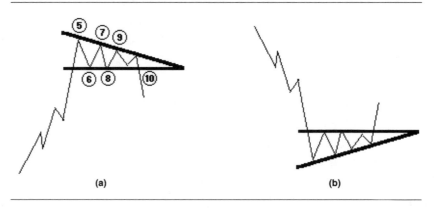

(a)   (b)

even lower one at Point 9. All the while, support has been firm. If you connect Points 6 and 8, and then extrapolate, you get a horizontal line. Now if you draw a trend line between Points 5 and 7 and extrapolate, what you come up with is a Descending Triangle. Let us try to figure out what is happening. As we said, support has remained steady. Yet every attempt to exceed the previous high has fallen shorter than the last. There seems to be a lack of confidence in this stock. Traders who regretted not selling at the previous peak are getting a little antsy and settling for less the next time. Traders settling for less is not a good sign. The likely outcome is a break low and a reversal of trend at Point 10. With the break low, you definitely want to see some high volume to confirm it.

Figure 4.7b is the other side of the coin, the reversal of a downtrend called an *Ascending Triangle*. Remember our model with its accumulation and distribution trading ranges. A serious difficulty with it was telling one range from the other. Let's say you are watching a trading range and have pegged it as a distribution phase. This range turns into an Ascending Triangle, which tends to contradict your prediction. Turning into a Descending Triangle would tend to confirm it. Of course the reverse is true when you think you are dealing with an accumulation phase. Furthermore, all these indications are opposite and backward when you are dealing with a Descending Triangle.

The most important thing to remember about reversal signals is that they never come with a guarantee. Only a fool goes straight from a reversal signal to her checkbook. There are a few mandatory stops along the way. They are called indicators. Check them out. That's what they are for.

continuation signals

Our first continuation signal is the *Isosceles Triangle*. In Figure 4.8a we have an uptrend that leads to a shrinking trading range. Notice that the triangle formed is neither ascending nor descending. Notice also that the two lateral sides are equal in length. A triangle with two equal sides is symmetrical and

---

figure 4.8   the Isosceles Triangle signal

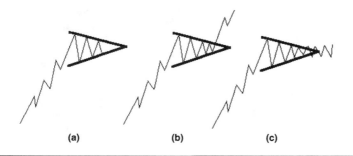

(a)   (b)   (c)

---

called an isosceles triangle. Thus, our continuation signal is called the Isosceles Triangle. Now you can believe that either all this is just a big coincidence, or that the world is starting to make sense. The choice is yours.

When you have a trend that ends in an Isosceles Triangle trading range, the likely outcome is a continuation of trend, as in Figure 4.8b If the original trend had been down, then after the Isosceles Triangle, the likely outcome would be a continuation of the downtrend. With this signal, you will usually see a decrease in volume accompany the decrease in range. Then when the trend resumes there should be a jump in volume. However, if the trading range continues beyond the triangle, as in Figure 4.8c, this is an indication that our signal is no signal at all. Anything can happen, and all bets are off.

Another continuation signal is illustrated in Figure 4.9a, the *Flag*. We start with an uptrend that ends in what looks like a flag. Not exactly a coincidence. This pattern is accompanied by

figure 4.9   the Flag and Pennant signals

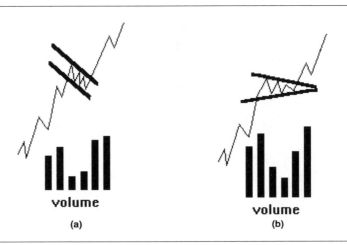

volume

(a)

volume

(b)

low volume. The *Pennant,* illustrated in Figure 4.9b is basically the same phenomenon, except it looks more like a pennant than a flag. In case you are wondering how to differentiate these signals from the triangle signals we discussed previously, you needn't worry. The Flag and Pennant have fewer up and down cycles, and they play themselves out over a much shorter period of time. They also have an even more severe shrinkage in volume.

Remember, in using our model that the crucial trick was being able to differentiate the accumulation phase from the distribution phase, and it was no easy trick at that. In themselves, they looked exactly alike, and if all their highs and lows did not precisely hit the support and resistance lines, they came very close. We mentioned then that these patterns were ideals, rarely seen in the real world. This seemed a disadvantage at the time. It isn't. The idiosyncrasies that accompany these trading ranges in the real world can sometimes be valuable clues in determining whether they are accumulation or distribution phases. In fact, these idiosyncrasies may coincide with those of the reversal and continuation signals we have just covered. When they do, you have yourself some weighty indicators.

chapter 5

buy and sell signals

it's true!!! buy low, sell high

It would now be worthwhile to review our buy and sell signals. First of all, remember a signal is just that and no more. Not one of the following buy or sell signals came down from Mount Sinai carved in stone. Never has anyone been struck by lightning for disregarding a buy or sell signal, even on a golf course, during a thunderstorm, taking cover under a tree. They are not signals to reach for your checkbook. They are signals to reach for your checklist of other possible signals, to quickly see if the relevant ones provide confirmation.

major buy signals

1. Buy on upturn off support as in Figure 5.1a.
2. Buy on break high as in Figure 5.1b.
3. Buy on pullback after break high as in Figure 5.1c.
4. Buy on last point of support in an uptrend, as in Figure 5.2a.
5. Buy on a break in resistance that indicates the reversal of a downtrend into an uptrend, as in Figure 5.2b.

figure 5.1   major buy signals I

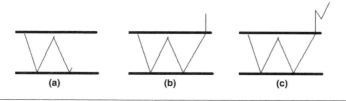

(a)   (b)   (c)

figure 5.2   major buy signals II

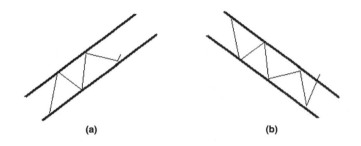

(a)   (b)

6. Buy when the Stochastic Oscillator is oversold and percentage *K* crosses percentage *D,* such as occurred at Point 5, Figure 5.3.

7. Buy when price is at a new low yet the RSI refuses to confirm any further drop by not going lower itself, as in Figure 5.4.

figure 5.3   major buy signals III

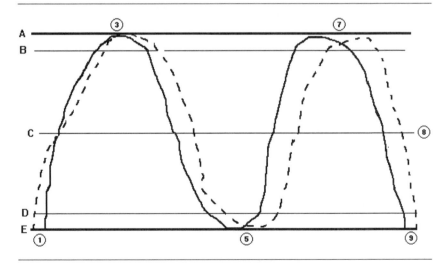

figure 5.4   major buy signals IV

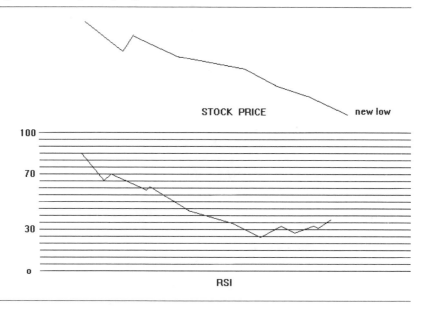

8. Using Quick Quote, buy on a negative to positive crossover, or when a stock rises above its opening price.

9. Buy a stock that is acting stronger than a declining S&P 500 when the S&P 500 Futures enters an uptrend, such as Stock Q in Figure 5.5.

major short signals

1. Short on downturn off resistance, as in Figure 5.6a.

2. Short on break low, as in Figure 5.6b.

3. Short after rally following break low, as in Figure 5.6c.

4. Short just after last point of supply during a downtrend, as in Figure 5.7a.

figure 5.5   major buy signals V

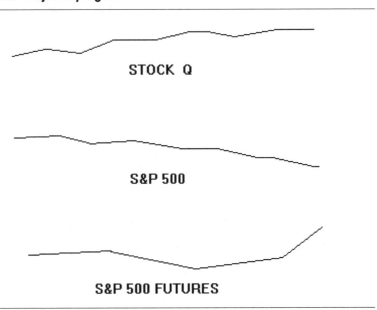

STOCK Q

S&P 500

S&P 500 FUTURES

5. Short on break in support indicating reversal of up-trend into downtrend, as in Figure 5.7b.

6. Short when Stochastic Oscillator is overbought and percentage *K* crosses percentage *D,* as occurs at Point 3, Figure 5.3.

figure 5.6   major short signals I

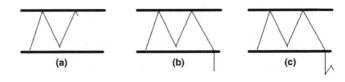

(a)   (b)   (c)

figure 5.7   major short signals II

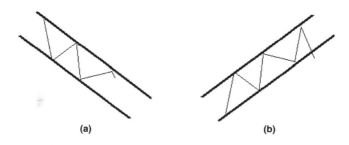

(a)   (b)

7. Short when stock price is rising to new high, but RSI is over 70 and refuses confirmation by rising any higher, as in Figure 5.8.

8. Using Quick Quote, short on a positive to negative crossover, or a drop in price below opening.

9. Short a stock that is acting weaker than an advancing S&P 500 when the S&P 500 Futures enters a downturn, as in Figure 5.9.

Not that I'm the least bit nervous about it, but before I turn you loose on the world with these buy and sell signals, perhaps it would be advisable to bring together what we have covered in this chapter within a controlled environment, that is, Fantasyland. Let's say you have been closely following the stock Rerecycle.com, Inc., ever since it changed its name from East Jersey Garbage Haulers. Well today, glued to the five-minute charts, you are less than excited, in fact you are mesmerized. Rerecycle.com, Inc. is locked inside a reinforced concrete, seemingly escape-proof trading range. You sit there wondering how many more damn times Rerecycle.com, Inc. is going to test its low. This stock has obviously got a support

figure 5.8   major short signals III

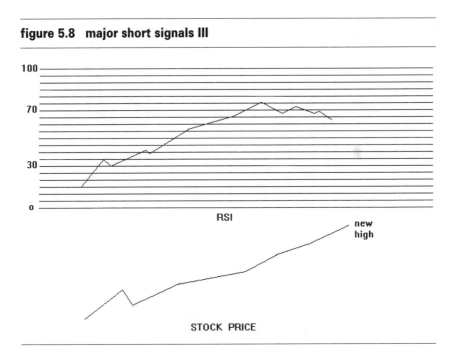

line made of enough concrete to shoe every stool pigeon and welsher alive. Which reminds you, if you do not want your own Gucci's encased in cement overshoes, then you had better pay off your bookie, fast. This payment could be facilitated by a nice little stock to sell short, because the S&P 500 has been in a steady downtrend from the opening bell, as in Figure 5.10a. Yet, in trying to find that one little stock to short, you have already been burned a half dozen times that day.

Rerecycle.com, Inc., is certainly no candidate to sell short. It has shown a lot of strength by not following the S&P 500 down. Wait a minute! You suddenly snap out of the day-long trance you had not even realized you were in. Maybe you have been playing the wrong game. This market may just

figure 5.9   major short signals IV

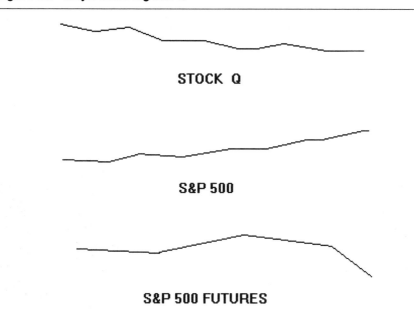

STOCK Q

S&P 500

S&P 500 FUTURES

figure 5.10   rerecycle.com

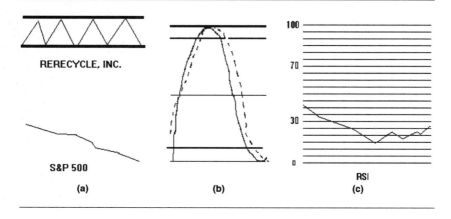

RERECYCLE, INC.

S&P 500

RSI

(a)   (b)   (c)

turn around. It could happen any minute. It is time to do some research.

You check the Stochastic on Rerecycle.com., and with very interesting results. The stock is oversold and percentage *K* has just crossed percentage *D,* as illustrated in Figure 5.10b. You cannot check the RSI fast enough. It is under 30 in "oversold territory," and it is turning upwards (see Figure 5.10).

Your pulse has quickened, your eyes are wide open, and you are ready to move. It is time to forget, at least for the moment, about looking for a stock to sell short. An upturn in the S&P Futures should mean a quick break high for Rerecycle, Inc. You are willing to bet on it, and bet heavy. Your fingers cannot work fast enough as you load up your order screen and wait for the S&P Futures to turn. Because if and when it does, what you will have, in technical terms, is a SCREAMING BUY!!!

chapter 6

breeds of stock traders

who's your daddy?

Four pure-blooded breeds account for a gigantic 2.479 percent of the stock trading population. Mongrelizations of infinite variety make up the remaining 97.521 percent. Fortunately, as it pertains to traders, breeding is a Pavlovian concept. Even a pit bull can be a poodle, merely by acting like one, and despite the trend in the opposite direction. The hard trick is to admit to yourself that the type of trader you really are may be quite different from the type of trader you think you are or want to be. Remember, this book is not written for traders who want to have a lot of fun, or meet interesting people, or make a lot of friends, that is, except as an adjunct to what I hope is your main objective in trading—making money. To make money, you have to keep from going broke. To keep from going broke, you better figure out fast what breed of trader you are. This means keeping records and determining the type or types of trading you find the most financially rewarding.

As we have said before, there are four basic *modus operandi* for the buying and selling of stock—day trading, overnight trading, swing trading, and position trading. As we have also said before, the basic distinction between these approaches is the timeframe involved. Though countless would-be traders have proven themselves equally inept at all four methods, very, very few traders have proven themselves equally adept at all four. The most successful traders know with certainty which methods, for them, mean more profits, and they more or less stick to these methods. They realize that gaining experience and knowledge about a troublesome method can only help up to a point. This is because each separate method requires its own mindset, focus, and approach. These factors are substantially dependant upon personality. Whenever you are faced with the choice of changing your methods or changing your personality, take my advice and junk your methods.

day traders

The day trader couldn't care less about the long haul. He or she buys a stock with the intention of selling it in a few minutes or a few hours, and absolutely no intention of keeping it overnight. The day trader expends a lot of energy while the market is open. He can easily make fifty trades in a day, many of course overlapping. He has to be something of a juggler, and the stocks he juggles are closer to eggs than rubber balls. If he makes a mistake, they do not bounce back up into his hand. And rest assured, he will make mistakes. They are inevitable. When the market closes, the day trader wants to slow down and recharge his batteries, at the very most do some low pressure research. No way does he want any stocks in his portfolio to worry about overnight.

The day trader's primary tools are the intraday five-minute and one-minute charts. He keeps a close eye on the S&P Futures Index, hoping that where it leads, the market will follow, with him one step ahead. He is far more interested in the price momentum of a stock than he is in its "true" value. The successful day trader has to be able to focus his concentration on his monitors. A moment's distraction can mean disaster. If you try day trading, and frequently find yourself staring at the screen wondering, "When did that happen?", this form of trading is not for you. Day trading does not require superhuman powers, but it does require the self-awareness to know when your concentration is flagging. At these times, it also requires the discipline to abandon your positions and your monitors, and of course it also requires the stamina to focus until you can do so.

The day trader searches for volatility like a vampire searching for blood. Predicting directions of volatility is his forte, or so he believes. He avoids thinly traded stocks. They are too easily manipulated and subject to unpredictable aberrations. The higher a stock's normal volume, the harder it is to manipulate. Keep in mind that volatility is a relative term. Most day traders are "scalpers," willing and satisfied to take their ¼ or ½ point profits. Of course many of them multiply these profits by taking on the added risk of buying on margin. Every once in a while, they also clean up or get cleaned out by some unexpectedly wide volatility. Of course, they could have protected themselves on the down side with buy stops and sell orders. Then again, there are those day traders that actually search out very high volatility stocks and the five- and ten-point profits that can be made on them.

overnight traders

The overnight trader is the rarest breed. Like the day trader, he or she takes and abandons positions within an extremely short timeframe and feels at home in front of one- and five-minute intraday charts. His most distinguishing personal characteristic is probably his ability to sleep like a log. Insomnia has never been this guy's problem. Generally, this breed of trader waits until between 3:00 and 4:00 P.M. to put on positions. If he thinks a stock is going to continue in an uptrend the next morning, or perhaps even gap open, he buys long. If he thinks it is going to continue in a downtrend, he sells short, hopefully with a buy stop. I should mention one other distinguishing characteristic of the overnight trader. He or she is not prone to oversleeping.

Ideally, overnight traders have closed out all their positions by 11:00 A.M. the next morning. This leaves them free to abandon their monitors until 2:30 P.M., possibly later. Allow me now to insert a serious word of warning. I realize that many of you readers that hibernate like bears at night, prefer long lunches, or are into illicit afternoon sexual affairs are now thinking that you have found not only your ideal method of trading stocks, but also the key to a happy future. Well, forgive me for pointing out that your suitability for this type of trading is not a matter of lifestyle preferences. The deciding factor should and ultimately will be: Can you make money as an overnight trader?

swing traders

The swing trader operates in a much longer timeframe than either the day or overnight trader, whole days at a time. He can actually have a life away from his monitors, even when the market is open. This breed is not interested in every little squiggle on the intraday charts. Sure, sometimes he sits glued to his monitors waiting for the next trade. Yet usually, the thing that brings him there, is some expectation drawn from the daily charts. The trends and trading ranges that interest him play out over a longer timeframe than those that are the bread and butter of the day trader or overnight trader. He also makes less trades than they do, and expects higher profits per trade.

A swing trader will play the trend of a stock, and if foolhardy or sophisticated enough to ignore the advice of this book, then contra trend the reactions. Of course, if he knows what is good for him, the swing trader will then waste no time getting back with the trend. He will also play those trading ranges that are wide enough to provide a worthwhile profit. This can mean buying and covering shorts on support, selling and selling short on resistance. If he is a sharp trader, he will have a good idea what type of trading range he is playing before he actually plays it. Remember, the likely resolution of an accumulation trading range is an uptrend, which is no place to be holding shorts. Conversely, the likely resolution of a distribution trading range is a downtrend—no place to be long. Therefore, your more prudent swing trader will stick to buying and selling in an accumulation phase, shorting and covering in a distribution phase.

position traders

The position trader, like the swing trader, is interested in the cumulative results of a day's trading, not the minute-by-minute volatility within that day. He chooses stocks for the long haul, uphill or down. Though his timeframe may stretch for years, a few weeks is also a possibility. A swing trader, ostensively trading with the trend, may very well try to grab a few points off a reaction. The position trader just guts out the reactions, waiting for the graphs to start moving in the right direction again. Merely because of the timeframe involved, do not assume that position traders are investors as opposed to speculators. That subjective judgment depends on numerous factors, the foremost being their choice of stocks.

Now that we are familiar with the *modus operandi* of our four pure breeds of stock traders, let's hunt us up a few. A good place to stalk them is their natural habitat, where they do their own stalking—the wild world of stock charts. The chart in Figure 6.1 is where you will find the position trader. In January he hears a rumor that Organic Bananas and Radishes is planning a hostile takeover of American Steel. Still, he has heard too many similar rumors that died stillborn to leap into a position before he looks. Looking doesn't tell him much. At Point 5, Organic Banana is stuck in a trading range. Some fast research points him toward the conclusion that this is an accumulation range. Still, even if it is, other factors, from microscopic insects to huge hurricanes can come into play preventing an uptrend. Yet he is tempted to take a position long and do so fast. Still, something vague holds him back. Sure bananas and steel are a natural fit, but he isn't so sure about radishes.

If our position trader could follow trading ranges for more than two minutes at a time without nodding off, he

figure 6.1   Organic Bananas and Radishes

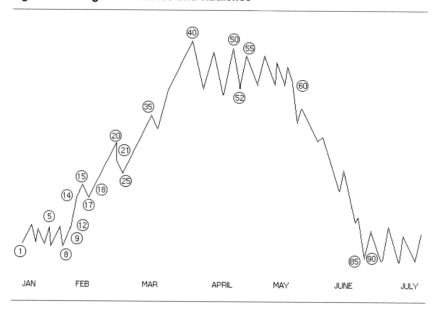

would probably do some day trading, too. He can't, so he won't. He can't walk away either. At Point 9, he decides to buy 1000 shares if Organic Banana breaks out of its trading range in the right direction and rises an additional two points, two points that no voracious day trader would give up without a fight. Our position trader has no intention of staring at his monitor in the meantime. Instead, his entry strategy consists of putting in a buy stop order, then taking his all-time favorite position at the stern of his all-time favorite fishing charter boat.

Sure enough, one week and sixty-four pounds of fish later, Organic Banana breaks out of its trading range and hits Point 12, thus setting off his buy stop. This happened of course while our trader was off fishing. By the time he found out, the stock had closed up another two points and he already had a two thousand dollar profit. So now he is in, and in for the long haul, expecting a sizeable return on investment. That leaves him with the problem of figuring the exchange rate between his paper profits and various available fishing charters.

At Point 20 on our graph, to our trader's pleasure, the takeover rumors prove true. To his displeasure, the "experts" question the fit. Share price plummets. Still, our trader is confident that the stock will recover. Something tells him that steel and bananas are too good a fit to be dragged down by radishes. Besides, it is definitely not his game to sell short on a reaction. Sure enough, two weeks later at Point 25 on our graph, for the first time in his tenure, the CEO of Organic Banana finally does something to rate his bloated salary and larcenous stock options. He announces a spinoff of the entire radish works. The "experts" swoon in approval.

Stock price takes off and our happy position trader holds on for the ride. He has no thoughts of doing anything else until Point 50. Here he finds himself in one more boring trading range. Now, if he were sure this was merely a holding pattern in a continued uptrend, he would be glad to hold on himself. Yet, there is too much evidence that this is a distribution trading range that will end in a downtrend. At Point 52, the next point of support, he decides to sell at a very handsome profit on the next point of resistance, which turns out to be Point 55.

It would take a long time to spend all his profits on fishing, so at the same time he sells his 1000 shares, he shorts 1000 shares. Incidentally, as a stop loss strategy, he also puts in a buy stop for an equal amount at two points over resistance. Sure enough, Organic Banana and Steel breaks support at Point 60. Our position trader ignores all reactions on the way down, and does not cover his short until Point 90. He picked a winner and stuck with it, long and short. Of course, he has also been known to pick losers. Still, he has never been know to sit glued to his monitors for days at a time.

A pure swing trader is not interested in holding a stock for four months, then selling it short and waiting two more months to cover that short. He attempts to make his money in a much shorter timeframe. Let us now return to the trading range between Points 1 and 8. The difference between support and resistance never amounts to much more than a point, and is often less than half that. This is too narrow a range to interest a swing trader. He has a feeling that this is an accumulation phase, but he is not sure enough to bet on it. The break in resistance reaches Point 14 before he is convinced that Organic Banana and Radishes is in a significant uptrend. Before he can act, the reaction between Points 15 and 17 renews his doubts. Still, he cannot resist the following upturn, buying 500 shares long at Point 18.

Remember, a pure swing trader does not hold positions for the long haul. Whereas a position trader ignores reactions such as that occurring between Points 20 and 25, the swing trader abandons his positions as soon as he can, in this case Point 21, doing so even though he believes rightly that this downturn is a temporary reaction, not a reversal of trend. According to our Rule 3, "Trade with the Trend," our trader should not sell short here, then cover that short as close as he can to the upturn at Point 25. Many successful swing traders would disagree with me. I stand by Rule 3. If you insist on getting more out of this uptrend, I would advise doubling your long positions as opposed to bucking the trend. My advice concerning the downtrend between Points 60 and 85 would be just the opposite. Trade with the trend by selling short and covering, without taking any long positions on the reactions. Returning to the other side of our chart, a swing trader would take another position long after Point 25 as soon as he thinks the reaction is over.

Trading ranges involve similar choices for the swing trader. First of all, let me emphasize again that the accumulation phase between Points 1 and 8 is too narrow to entice him. However, the first half of the distribution phase between Points 40 and 52 offers some mouth-watering ranges of between two to three points. Again, many swing traders both buy on support and short on resistance no matter whether the trading range in an accumulation or distribution phase. Also again, I recommend against this. An accumulation phase ends in an uptrend, no place to be caught selling short. A distribution phase ends in a downtrend, no place to be caught holding long. My advice is to first determine the type of trading range with which you are dealing. Buy long or sell short accordingly. Do not do both.

Looking at Figure 6.1 again, we see that with this particular stock, the position trader took and abandoned only two positions in six months. The swing trader made numerous trades, holding positions for periods from days up to weeks. Now the day trader, depending on his indicators, could have made hundreds of trades all over the chart, picking up a half point here and a quarter point there. The overnight trader, limited to one trade a day in a particular stock, could have made more trades than the swing trader but far less than the day trader. Obviously, the longer you hold a position, the greater the necessity that it be profitable and the larger margin of profit necessary to justify the trade.

As stated previously, rarely does a stock trader limit himself to only one of the four methods of trading. Still, successful traders usually focus their efforts on one or two approaches. Each of the four methods requires its own skills, some acquirable some innate. It pays to find out where your skills lie, and to find out fast. If you are the strong-willed type, spelled *s t u b b o r n,* convinced that you are equally skilled at all four methods, and you are willing to spend all of your time away from the monitor doing the necessary research, then go right ahead. However, allow me to mention, that even if you do make enough money to buy a life, you will not have any time to live it. My advice is to concentrate your efforts and capital on the stock trading method you find most financially rewarding.

chapter 7

trading stocks online

"this program has performed an illegal operation"—Windows®

You have probably been wondering irritably if the online part of *Technical Trading Online* consists solely of one word in the title. In fact, some of you more suspicious readers may have even decided that putting online in the title was just a trendy gimmick to get you to buy this book. Well, I can say in all honesty, that in your case it obviously worked.

Actually, there has been a cleverly hidden, integral online component throughout this book. To trade stocks technically, you need technical input—graphs, indicators, analysis, and other necessary data. Were it not for online sources, this would all be unavailable in a timely enough manner to the vast majority of stock traders. The next few chapters will show you the extent of online sources and how to tap them. I do have to mention the reason why this information is largely segregated into a few chapters, as opposed to being integrated throughout the book. I am confident that the material contained in *Technical Trading Online* up to this point will be relevant and useful to stock traders for many years to come. However, much of the material in the next few chapters will be outdated by the time this book goes into print, not to mention by the time you read it. In fact, for simplicity and sanity's sake, I will not even note where a few of the generalizations that I will make already have their exceptions. To keep up to date with what is happening online, you have to get online and you have to stay there. Despite this unfortunate fact, the following material should prove helpful in that process.

The past few years have brought a revolution to the business of buying and selling stocks. Surprisingly, the newer methods by which much of this business is now conducted were more a necessary cause of this revolution than a result of it. There are basically three ways to buy and sell stocks. The traditional, and still important way, is through a personal broker. The next step, a technical one, is online, substituting a computer interface for the personal broker, and in the long run, probably replacing the personal broker as we know him. The third way, technically the state of the art, is Electronic Direct Access Trading (EDAT). Our concern in this book is method number two, online trading. However, to best understand this method, it is helpful to know how it differs from the other two methods.

When dealing with a broker, the customer meets him in person or speaks to him on the telephone. This provides an opportunity for the broker to offer his opinion on the market as a whole and a few stocks in particular. The novice trader often lived and died by this advice. Since the broker makes his income from fees that are based on the volume and value of the stocks his clients buy and sell, it is to his advantage to keep his clients living, or at the very least, to make sure they die slowly. However, it is also to his advantage if his clients do a lot of buying and selling. What we have here is an inherent conflict of interest. Now I am sure no broker ever consciously churned his client's accounts, but, human nature being what it is, there may have been a rare few who, when in a personal financial pinch, might have honestly convinced themselves that it was to their client's advantage to sell or buy one hell of a lot of stock fast. There have also been dark rumors that on occasion, certain brokers have actually overhyped certain stocks to raise prices and unload their own holdings at a handsome profit. Let us hope these rumors are nothing more than unfounded lies.

The online trader is a breed apart. He has no time to waste on small talk with brokers, no trust in the spoken word, whether for scuttlebutt or for making a trade. He also spends less money on broker fees—online charges being much less than those of full service brokers. He does his research and gets his information online at the speed of his modem, sometimes so fast he ends up drowning in it. No, our online trader, and make no mistake, he is the hero of this book, would rather look at his computer monitor, making his trades face to interface, until Windows freezes over, which seems to be more and more often with each new edition.

On the brighter side, if you pay close attention to the rest of this book, you just may make enough money trading stocks online to pay other people to look at your computer screens for you.

I will return to online trading in the next chapter, but first for some very important reasons, we must discuss Electronic Direct Access Trading (EDAT). For four not so important reasons, we shall keep our discussion as short as possible. First, the subject of EDAT can get extremely complicated. Second, what is true today is likely to be outdated information tomorrow. Third, EDAT trading is not the subject of this book. Fourth, it is possibly the subject of my next book. Though online trading is much faster than trading through a personal broker, EDAT trading is faster still. In both EDAT and online trading, you find yourself staring at a monitor. What you see on those monitors may also be similar. Do not be fooled. It is what's behind the monitor that makes the difference. Online, you are connected to your broker through the Internet. You are not buying the stock yourself. You are asking your broker to acquire it for you. Often, instead of doing this himself, he sells your order to a middleman. In addition, download times can drive you nuts. In crisis situations, they can even drive you to violent acts, not to mention naughty language. With EDAT, you are usually connected by a dedicated phone line with direct access to the market. You buy the stocks yourself, almost instantaneously, with mouse and keyboard. Downloads are lightning fast.

These speed advantages accelerate not only the buying and selling of stock, but also the researching of stocks—from quotes, to charts, to breaking news. In business, time is money. In the stock market, time is often the difference between solvency and insolvency. And the faster you get to the market, the more likely you are to get your target price, and in fact to complete your trade at all. However, the actual value of speed varies according to conditions. News that breaks at six o'clock in the evening may be just as valuable anytime over the next nine hours, up until the market opens. The day trader, making his living off minute, temporary price fluctuations, needs his information instantly, or at least as fast as anyone else is getting it. A seasoned EDAT day trader would feel very constrained online, and possibly, shortly, insolvent. The position trader, buying a mutual fund for the long haul, can walk back from the water cooler slowly enough to keep from spilling half the cup down the front of his pants. A day trader who can make money online, can probably make more money on EDAT. He or she should perhaps try it, but there are added costs and dangers we will discuss later.

Online trading is most often done from the home or office, and this office is nearly always one where the online trader is supposed to be doing something other than trading stocks. The fact that this online trader, by his very trading, is often disposing of the ill-gotten gains he is accruing for supposedly doing the job he is in fact ignoring while instead trading stocks, lends such a sense of elegant symmetry to this tiny aspect of our limitless, wondrously chaotic universe that it would tend to make even the most vicious murderer, rapist, stock broker, or even IRS agent believe, for at least a brief instant, in the existence of God.

A Level II screen is an expensive option that can benefit all traders, especially day traders. In addition to showing the highest price bid for a stock and lowest price asked, it also gives you the next levels of bids and asks. This better enables you to gauge a stock's strength. With practice, you will gain skill in judging which bids and offers are legitimate and which are bluffs.

EDAT trading, especially day trading, can be done remotely, in the home or office. However, a full home setup can cost you from a few hundred to a thousand dollars a month. For this reason, EDAT trading is almost always conducted on site, in an office designed especially for this activity. Traders sit side by side in rows, staring at numerous monitors that display real time stock information. In rare cases, these traders are risking other people's money for a percentage of profits. Most often, they are trading their own money, and some of these traders work under the umbrellas of Limited Liability Corporations (LLCs). Their transaction charges are fractions of standard personal brokers' fees. The funds of all traders are comingled, thus allowing leverage of 10 to 1 or more instead of the standard 2 to 1, commonly referred to as Regulation T margins.

The trader contributes his share of the corporation's capital, let's say $50,000, and theoretically he is a partner. And if the trader really believes this, he is way too naive to go outside his house unless accompanied by an adult. Do not worry. He won't be outside for long. High leverage is not a tool for beginners. In no time, bad trades will have gobbled up his $50,000, and he will be back home, safe and insolvent where he belongs. Partners of LLCs are in effect clients of them. Only in one extreme case does theory meet reality, making all the traders of an LLC in fact partners. That case is bankruptcy. Rest assured there are numerous safeguards to prevent one of your high-rolling partners from wiping out the entire firm's capital. Also rest assured that these safeguards have not always worked.

A far more common problem is individual traders getting wiped out, some of course deservedly. Don't be surprised if the SEC clamps down by tightening requirements on LLCs. However, this won't eliminate another pitfall of trading by mouse and keyboard. Computer monitors have a way of mesmerizing people. Mesmerized people make silly mistakes. In the stock market, one silly mistake can mean financial ruin. Let's say you are having a good day, but nothing compared to the fantastic night that preceded it. And let's say that not a single minute of this fantastic night was wasted on sleep. And let's say one more thing, that you are not one of these infamous, greedy, beady-eyed day traders. No sir, not you. One more little trade and you will cash in and go home for a nap. As you decide this, it occurs to you that never in your whole life have you traded a single share of IBM. You've always wanted to. There is something about those three pretty letters. They mean strength, intelligence, and most important, class. It's time you owned a thousand shares of Big Blue. No, it has been a good day. Make it ten thousand shares, with a ¼ stop for safety's sake. You start tapping on your keyboard, thinking, "This EDAT is easy as marbles." Unfortunately, you should have been thinking about numbers not marbles, because you just bought one hundred thousand shares instead of ten thousand. Wouldn't you know it, IBM hits your stop just as you realize this. Just then you realize something else too. Trading on EDAT may be as easy as shooting marbles, but EDAT has no equivalent of calling, "Slipsies!"

If you can't make money trading without the advantages of EDAT and a Level II screen, do not deceive yourself into thinking that they are the only difference. However, if you are successful without them, then there is a very good chance that you can be more successful with them.

I think it appropriate to end this chapter with the admonition that while trading online or through EDAT may facilitate the making of your fortune in far less time than this would have taken through a personal relationship with a broker, these methods of trading can facilitate equally well the quick loss of your fortune. Of course, if for you profit and loss are minor considerations compared to time saved, then this admonition should not concern you in the least. Then again, neither should this book you are reading. Allow me to remind you that *Technical Trading Online* is written for people who are interested in making money through the purchase and sale of stocks.

chapter 8

setting up your monitor

"you don't know jack"
meets "doom" meets "winky dink"

The following chapter is probably a good place to oil and get the rust off of your speed-reading skills. If you do not have a monitor yet, then you will probably forget most of this chapter before you get one. If you already have a monitor, and it is set up, you may want to keep your monitor the way it is. However, there is nothing in this chapter that in itself will cause you or your financial statement any permanent damage. In fact, there is a good chance it contains a few sentences here and there that will prove both new and valuable. In short, if the word "short" can still be applied, this chapter is to be read quickly, certainly not studied and memorized.

First, let me state that if there is any correlation between particular screen setups and trading success, I haven't found it. Second, individual screen setups probably vary as much as individual DNA. In setting up your monitor, the objective should be to find the arrangement that is the most effective, comfortable, quickest, easiest, and safest to use. If I have given you the impression that setting up your screens is a job to be taken lightly, I have given you the wrong impression. A brain's output is dependant on its input. Unfortunately, our society places too low a value upon quality input. Perhaps this is because too many people, many of them stock traders, have meat grinders for minds. Superior input is not foolproof, but it certainly does no harm. More to the point, in the best of all possible worlds, every buy and sell decision you make should be based upon, or at the very least confirmed by, the information you see on your quote, graph, and other screens.

Now it is not absolutely necessary to have a different monitor for each screen. All you need is a mouse to point and click from one screen to another. In fact, this is the best that most online brokers can offer you (at least as of five minutes ago). However, you can also subscribe to an information service as I prefer to do. Information services can be very, very expensive. It takes an experienced stock trader to get his or her money's worth. Besides, the novice trader can go online and get more information than he can digest for free. Using an information service involves using at least two monitors attached to one PC with a splitter card, or better yet, two PCs. One monitor will show information about the market, arranged to enable quick and easy analysis. We shall refer to the screens on this monitor as quote or graph screens, though they will actually display much more. The other monitor is connected online to a broker and usually displays order entry screens.

One quote screen can contain all the information we need, and many traders find just such a setup sufficient. I don't. I like to see my graphs large, and I do not like them overlapping and covering up other information. For this reason, I set up my information monitor so I can toggle between printed information and graphs.

Setting up your quote screen, you have to keep two objectives in mind—displaying all necessary data and doing so in a simple, uncrowded, and easy to use format. Unfortunately, these are two very conflicting objectives that I myself have yet to completely reconcile. Unless you prove more successful, you too will have to compromise on both objectives. There is no point in giving you an illustration of a well set up quote screen. All the free online and broker supplied screens have different setups and options. None of them are capable of providing all the information I consider necessary on a quote screen, nor do all the pay services. Instead, I will go over what

I find necessary, some of it only available from pay services. The novice is surely better off starting without this added expense. It will take a while before he or she even learns to take full advantage of all data available from free sources.

The first necessary display we shall discuss is the time. Even the most mystical stock trader finds it helpful to know when the market is about to open or close, and whether he is trading during regular or extended hours. Day traders who fade the opening want to be back trading with the trend by 10:30 A.M. at the latest. They also want to avoid the market between 12:00 and 2:00 P.M., when volume dries up. Most of all, they want to be a flat, in other words, positionless by 4:00 P.M.

A comprehensive list of market indicators is essential. Though it is always tempting to start by checking individual stocks, your analysis must begin with an examination of the market as a whole, thus providing a context in which to examine each particular stock's price and movement. Table 8.1 provides a list of indicators and their corresponding symbols.

Once you have a feel for the market as a whole, it is time to examine the group indexes, again before you check individual stocks. Obviously, if you are interested in an oil stock, you should also be interested in the XOI, the oil index. Less obviously, if the oil index is moving in a different direction than nearly all the other indexes, it is definitely worthwhile to know if and how this will effect your position. Sometimes you can even detect relationships between specific indexes. A change in the CEX, the chemical index, may foreshadow a change in the XOI or vice versa. The group indexes themselves should be listed together as a group. If you want each index listed along with the stocks that comprise it, then list them in both places.

Table 8.1 market indicators

Symbol	Meaning
INDP	Dow Jones Industrial Average, e.g., 1056
INDU	Change in INDP, e.g., +52
TRAN	Dow Jones Transportation Average
UTIL	Dow Jones Utility Average
COMP.Q	Nasdaq Composite Average
SPX	Standard & Poor's 500 Index
SPX/N	Change in SPX
SPU.Z	Standard & Poor's Futures Contracts
SPU/N	Change in SPU.Z
IADV	Advancing Issues N.Y. Stock Exchange
IDEC	Declining Issues N.Y. Stock Exchange
VOLU	Total Volume N.Y. Stock Exchange
UVOL	Total up Volume N.Y. Stock Exchange
DVOL	Total Down Volume N.Y. Stock Exchange
VOLQ	Nasdaq Total Volume
TICK	Net Ticks plus or minus N.Y. Stock Exchange
TRIN	Traders Index

If possible, for easy identification of trends, advancing indexes should be listed in green and declining in red. Table 8.2 is a list of group indexes and their symbols.

Most of your quote screen should be taken up by all relevant stocks listed separately by group. Opposite each stock should be its current price, again in red and green if possible. This will facilitate finding the groups and the stocks within them most in line with the trend of the market as a whole. If nearly all the stocks in a group are the same color, they get your attention. Of even greater interest is a group's switching from predominantly one color to another.

In a convenient place, you should also list all stocks in which you have taken positions or are thinking of taking positions. The prices will be listed opposite them. If available, you

Table 8.2   group indexes

Symbol	Meaning
HCX	Health Care
DRG	Drug
BKX	Financial #1
BIX	Financial #2
XCI	Technology #1
CEX	Chemical
RLX	Retail
XOI	Oil
XAU	Metals
IUX	Insurance
SOX	Technology #2
CMR	Consumers
CYC	Cyclical

should also show a more detailed quick quote or streamer containing the one or two stocks you are most interested in at the moment. If these sustain your interest, then the next step is to take a look at some graphs. This is usually accomplished by clicking a mouse to overlay some graphs or by switching to a graph screen.

Each graph screen usually contains graphs pertaining to one particular stock, as in Figure 8.1. If possible, it pays to develop standard graphs, incorporating the same indexes and indicators in the same places. This enables almost reflexive analysis with a minimum of errors. At the very least, try to use a standard graph for each group of stocks such as airlines or chemical companies. Graphs can and should be modified to gain different perspectives.

If enough space remains, and you are into status symbols, you can list a couple of popular option indexes. The Major Market Index (XMI) is made up of 20 stocks. It closely mirrors

figure 8.1 Candlestick graph

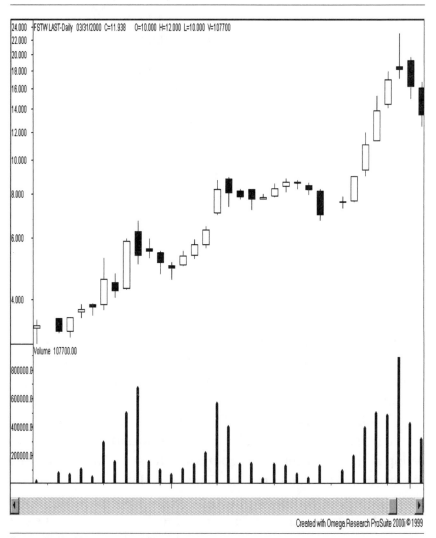

Source: Used with permission of Omega Research.

the Dow Jones Industrial Average. The Standard & Poor's 100 Index (OEX) closely mirrors the Standard & Poor's 500 Index. This explanation should be enough to impress any novice who asks. However, in case someone that does understand the intricacies of option trading starts discussing these indexes, you might want to bone up enough to hold your own, or at least to fake it.

chapter 9

buying and selling online

"our business is built on personal relationships"—motto of now defunct brokerage house (the name of which escapes me)

All online brokers have different stock order screens. Even the terminology sometimes varies. Be careful. Do not assume your next order screen works like your last one, or like the following example, graciously provided by Datek Online (datek.com). That said, you can begin your next speed reading drill.

As soon as you are seriously considering taking a position in a particular stock, it is time to move to the stock order screen. As I said, there is no standard screen among brokers. Even a single broker's order screen may have a few variations to enable different activities, such as placing a stock order, placing an option order, and modifying an order.

Datek refers to the order screen in Figure 9.1 as its Quotes and Trades screen. Right away we see the date, time, and some indexes in the upper left-hand corner. Let us say you are considering taking a position in Firstwave Technologies, Inc. You type *FSTW* in the *Enter Symbol* box, and click on *Go*. A quick quote appears across the center of our screen. You are interested but not sold. Just above and on the right side of the quick quote you have some pull down menus for news, charts, and research. Trips to all three screens prove helpful. You are now sold, deciding to buy 1000 shares. With your mouse, click on the *Buy* circle in the lower left-hand corner, type *1000* in the *Quantity* box, and type *FSTW* in the *Symbol* box. Skip the *Price* box for a minute and go to the *Order Type* box. This is a pull-down menu with four choices: Market, Limit, Stop Market, Stop Limit. A market order buys the stock at the market price when the order is received. Choosing this option means you do not go back and fill in the *Price* box. This is the only way to be sure you get the stock, but we cannot be sure how much you will have to pay.

figure 9.1　Datek order screen

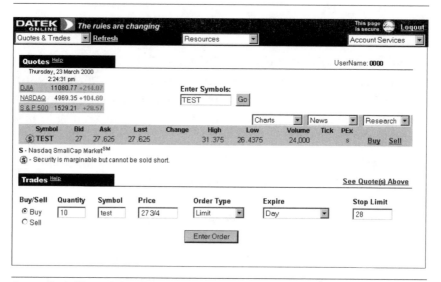

Source: Used with permission of Datek Online.

Usually, the price will be close to the quick quote, but a sudden run on the stock is a dangerous possibility. Only the very experienced trader should use a market order. Anyone else should stick to a limit order. Let us say FSTW is selling at $20. You choose *Limit* from the pull-down menu, then go back to the *Price* box and type in $21. This means you will still get the 1000 shares for market price, as long as market price does not exceed $21. If, when your order is received, share price exceeds $21, you will not get the stock, but in the meantime, you do not have to worry about losing the farm.

The third choice in the *Order Type* box is *Stop Market.* One circumstance in which you might make this choice is if FSTW is about to test its resistance line at 22. You feel that if it breaks resistance, the stock will go into a markup phase. To catch this ride, choose *Stop Market* from the *Order Type* box, then go back to the *Price* box and type in 22⅜, for example. Your order will lie dormant unless the stock price hits 22⅜, then it will be filled at market. This is dangerous!!! If FSTW does go into a markup phase, there is no telling at what price your order will be filled. For this reason, I recommend stop limit orders. In the *Order Type* box, choose *Stop Limit.* Leave 22⅜ in the *Price* box, and this will remain your activation price. However, now move to the last box on the right, the *Stop Limit* box, and type in a price ceiling such as 24. Now if FSTW does break resistance, your buy order will be activated at 22⅜. If your order cannot be filled before the price rises above $24, again you won't get the stock but you won't have to worry about losing the farm in the meantime.

The pull-down menu in the *Expire* box also gives you four choices: Day, GTC, Day+Ext. Hours, GTC+Ext. Hours. Choosing *Day* automatically cancels an order still unfilled at the end of the day. You make this choice as opposed to *GTC.* GTC stands for "Good 'Till Cancelled" (actually good for 30 calendar days, with Datek), a choice that should only be selected after consideration of how often you find yourself in your garage, trying to remember why the hell you went out there in the first place. We ignored the choices with *+Ext. Hours* because this means the trade can take place after normal trading hours, and I have no intention of getting into that. So click on the *Enter Order* button, *read* and fill out the confirmation page, and then leave Datek's Quotes and Trades page behind.

chapter 10

online information sources

**mortgage your house
and follow your mouse**

The question is, "What's so great about online information sources?" The answer is, "Just about everything." For example, take charts. Today, any amateur, connected online to any of numerous Web sites, can bring up at no charge, just about any stock chart he or she cares to see. A few years ago, these charts were available only to professional traders. Now also available online are myriad sources of information on how to interpret these charts.

Charts are just the beginning. Online and for free you can find original and reprinted news articles, research, analysis, instruction, training, actual courses, ratings of software, ratings of services, ratings of Web sites, tax information that will help you save money, tax information to help you fill out your return, tax information that could easily get you thrown out of H&R Block, tax information that could probably get you thrown into jail, portfolio services that keep track of all your holdings no matter how vast, E-mail addresses, E-mail newsletters, E-mail bulletins, beeper notification if among many other things your stock hits a specified price, real-time quotes, for the weak-hearted delayed quotes, chat rooms, message boards, online stores containing 100 percent junk, online stores containing only 99 percent junk, and most important, links to an endless chain of other links. If you don't find all this exciting, then obviously you have actually been online at least once in your life.

Now is the appropriate time for me to list all the most useful Web sites, and to give a detailed description of what they each have to offer. Unfortunately, I ain't the appropriate author to do said dirty work. Besides, much of this information would probably be outdated by the time I typed the period at the end of the sentence containing it. Instead, what you are going to get is an incomplete list of useful Web sites, more or less connected by some awkward sentences containing some truly interesting information. I recommend you give each mentioned Web site a quick, superficial examination, then go through them very thoroughly, one by one. Follow your mouse and really get into them. Click on every page available. Avoid links to other sites until you know just about everything each Web site has to offer. Then, before you check out your next Web site, shave off your beard, take a shower, and get something to eat. It's a fact, anyone who really gets into any of these Web sites does so at their own risk. I will gladly tell you something that AOL never would: Many a Web surfer of these pages I am about to mention has disappeared without a trace. They have gotten so far into them that if they have in fact ever emerged, it was on the other side of the universe. Believe me when I say, black holes have nothing on Yahoo!Finance. Enough said about our first Web site, finance.yahoo.com.

Let's delve even deeper into our next Web site, TheStreet.com—a fine source of online information. TheStreet.com's news items have the reputation of being up to the minute and free of hype. Its contributors have a reputation for intelligence and insight, if not big portfolios. One of them, Gary B. Smith, a highly respected trader, contributes columns on technical analysis. I recommend that you read him.

We should get away from this Web site before we sink into it, but first allow me to give you one example of how useful it can be. Let's say you are looking for your first online broker, or perhaps you are not satisfied with your present one. You could try that old tried and true method for getting bad advice: Ask a friend. You could research it on the Web until you have either found a broker or gotten too dizzy to continue. However, if you were a faithful visitor to TheStreet.com, you could have solved this problem my way, the lazy way. Sure enough they had a reader's poll. It not only ranked online brokers overall, it ranked them on 17 separate criteria in case some of these were of particular importance to you. Not only that, it divided the ranking into two groups mysteriously referred to as "leagues." This way, the smaller brokers in League B did not get overpowered by the larger ones in League A, which of course received more votes. With TheStreet.com's gracious, if self-serving, permission, I have included both of these rankings in Figures 10.1 and 10.2.

What other goodies can you find free online? A lot more than you can digest. For example, instead of just knowing the highest bid and the lowest ask for a stock, it would be helpful to see the other bids and asks right down the line. No way are you going to stumble upon a Level II screen online. One of those will cost you money. However, at isld.com and also through various links, you can bring up the ECN Island's limit order book, which is as close as you are going to get to a Level II screen for free. On thinly traded stocks, Island's order book will be of very limited value. Still, on high volume stocks it can sometimes give you a fairly close approximation of a Level II screen. The closeness of Island's narrowest bid and ask to that of the market's as a whole is some indication of what you are getting.

There is one sure fire way to save some money by taking advantage of an online resource. Instead of doing your experimenting with the milk money, do it with Monopoly money on an online trading simulator such as can be found at sandbox.com /business/ or cybercorp.com/simulators/. However, keep in mind that a simulator is no more than that, and success on one in no way guarantees success in the stock market. Still, simulators are a no lose proposition. Even if they teach you nothing, the time they keep you away from the real market will most likely save you some real moolah.

figure 10.1 TheStreet.com's rankings of large online brokers

League A Rankings							
Criteria*	Datek (1)	Fidelity (2)	Schwab (3)	DLJdirect (4)	Ameritrade (5)	E*Trade (6)	TD Waterhouse (7)
Reliability: access even in times of heavy volume	3	2	4	1	5	6	7
Real-time quotes	1	5	2	3	6	4	7
Fast order confirmation	1	2	4	3	5	6	7
Easy account administration & portfolio tracking	2	4	1	3	6	5	7
Customer service	4	1	2	5	3	6	7
Best execution price	1	2	3	4	6	7	5
Easy to implement complex trades	1	4	2	3	6	5	7
Low commissions	1	4	7	6	2	5	3
Real-time market & company news	4	5	3	1	6	2	7
Investment research	6	4	1	2	7	3	5
IPO Availability	7	3	4	1	6	2	5
Breadth of investment product offerings	7	1	2	4	6	3	5
Level II Nasdaq quotes	3	2	5	4	6	1	7
Email Alerts	5	6	3	1	4	2	7
Easy options trading	7	5	3	1	4	2	6
After-hours trading	1	5	4	3	6	2	7
Banking services	5	2	1	6	7	4	3
Bond trading	7	2	3	1	6	4	5

*In order of importance to readers. League A brokers received more than 650 votes each. League B brokers received between 72 and 312.

[Print]

League A rankings   League A scores   Close Window   League B rankings   League B scores

Source: Reprinted with permission of TheStreet.com, www.thestreet.com.

Just five of many more interesting and worthwhile sites are ragingbull.com, fool.com, wallstreetcity.com, marketguide.com, and cbs.marketwatch.com. Following links on all the sites I have mentioned will lead you to many other sites. Listing and describing Web sites, especially new ones, has become standard operating procedure for newspaper columnists whenever they can't or are too lazy to think of something really worthwhile to write about. Also, asking friends and acquaintances can turn you on to some hot sites. Finding valuable information online will never be a problem for you. Finding the stamina to absorb it all might.

figure 10.2   TheStreet.com's rankings of small online brokers

TheStreet.com - Netscape

League B Rankings

Criteria[1]	Dreyfus (1)	Brown (2)	ScoTTrade (3)	Merrill (4)	MSDW (5)	Vanguard (6)	NDB (7)	SureTrade (8)	Am Ex (9)	Quick & Reilly (10)
Reliability: access even in times of heavy volume	1	3	6	2	5	4	10	8	7	9
Real-time quotes	3	1	4	10	2	5	7	6	9	8
Fast order confirmation	1	2	5	3	7	4	6	10	9	8
Easy account administration & portfolio tracking	1	7	6	2	3	5	4	10	8	9
Customer service	5	6	3	1	4	2	9	10	8	7
Best execution price	1	2	3	4	6	5	7	9	8	10
Easy to implement complex trades	1	2	3	9	4	6	5	7	10	8
Low commissions	5	1	3	7 (tie)	10	9	6	2	4	7 (tie)
Real-time market & company news	4	10	8	1	2	9	5	3	7	6
Investment research	7	10	8	1	2	9	4	3	6	5
IPO Availability	6	8	7	2	1	10	4	3	9	5
Breadth of investment product offerings	4	10	8	2	3	1	7	9	6	5
Level II Nasdaq quotes	4	10	2	1	5	8	3	6	9	7
Email alerts	9	10	5	3	2	8	1	6	4	7
Easy options trading	1	2	5	4	3	8	7	9	10	6
After-hours trading	1	10	7	5	2	4	3	6	8	9
Banking services	7	8	10	1	4	3	5	9	2	6
Bond trading	5	10	6	1	2	3	4	9	8	7

[1]In order of importance to readers. League A brokers received more than 660 votes each. League B brokers received between 72 and 312.

[Print]

League A rankings   League A scores   Close Window   League B rankings   League B scores

Source: Reprinted with permission of TheStreet.com, www.thestreet.com.

The stock trader trying to make use of online resources invariably comes up against two problems:

1. Finding relevant information and
2. Being overwhelmed by irrelevant information.

Fortunately, there are some find and filter computer programs that eliminate this problem. Unfortunately, they can create another problem for the stock trader—being overwhelmed by relevant information. Often, when you install these programs on your computer, you are given the choice of a minimum setup with check boxes to add more complex functions and information. I recommend mastering the minimum capabilities of a program until you are completely comfortable with them. You can add the extra bells, whistles, and fog horns later, one by one. For example, you just bought a program that serves up real-time market data, both daily and intraday. If you have survived so far without real-time intraday data, you can survive another few weeks without it. In the meantime, use the unfamiliar computer program with the daily data so familiar to you. I realize this sounds like common sense, but the common mistake of doing just the opposite proves it isn't.

If you really want to get technical about technical trading online, then you should probably get some software to assist you. Omega Research's ProSuite 2000i is a consistently top-rated example. Let us just say that almost everything it does, which is a lot, revolves around helping the user develop, test, perfect, and implement trading systems.

For example, you are on the lookout for long positions in stocks that have stochastics giving buy signals and RSIs in the oversold zone, during full moons. However, your last few systems have not only left you and kept you broke, they have cost your millionaire father-in-law even more money. He is in no mood to talk to you, forget about back you. ProSuite can help. It can program far, far more complicated indicator criteria, along with myriad entrance and exit determinants. Not only can it locate the stocks you are looking for, it can E-mail or beep you every time it succeeds. Unfortunately, it cannot talk your father-in-law into backing you. However, it can certainly help you to do so.

There is no way of being certain how your system will do in the future. Still, ProSuite can test how it would have done in the past—back five, ten, even thirty years—and come up with detailed, dollar and cents results that you can shove in your father-in-law's face. Don't worry if ProSuite comes up with results that your father-in-law would shove right back in your own face. A quick switching of variables, in this case from full moon to new moon, can cut your losses in half, to about the size of the national debt. The addition of only one or two more indicators will surely have you showing a profit. Pardon us if we move on and leave you staring at the ProSuite screen in Figure 10.3.

You must have noticed that when I mentioned the availability of information online in this chapter, I never once inserted

figure 10.3　Prosuite screen

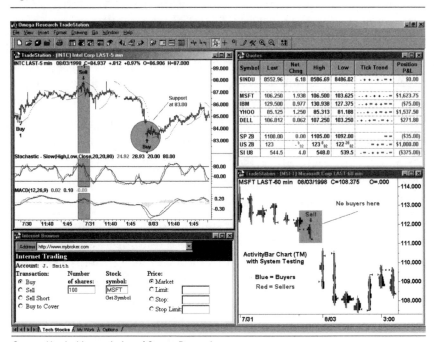

Source: Used with permission of Omega Research.

the word "good" before the word "information." Ah, I wish I could have. Unfortunately, we must end this chapter with a valuable yet dirty little nugget of fact: A significant portion of the information available online can be hazardous to your financial health. Alas, the printed word carries much too much weight with some people, even when that print comes over the Internet. Some novice traders take positions because of tips they receive in chat rooms or off message boards. They would have completely ignored most of these tips if they had been given in person. Remember, you too can be a message board guru, even if you are homeless, which some of these tipsters probably are or doubtless will be. And if someone's tips don't pan out, all he has to do is change his online alias, or at the most, his message board. Think about the reasons people give tips to complete strangers, even your own reasons. Think hard. Qualifying for sainthood didn't come to mind, did it?

Anyone with the memory of a turnip will be amazed how often "legitimate news" from supposedly reputable sources turns out to be misinformation, not to mention hype. People just don't seem to derive any inferences from the fact that the biggest slimeball from back in high school is now a hotshot reporter. Hell, by comparison with him, even most of today's stock brokers and lawyers were straight arrows then. Ethics aside, they also had way more brains.

Analysis could be just as dangerous as "news," if not for the fact that most traders either ignore it completely or take it to mean whatever they want it to mean. However, you True Believers ready to live and die by the last piece of analysis that you read should keep one interesting fact in mind. If you can hold off on taking a position just long enough to do some more research on the good old Internet, you can probably find some equally impressive analysis saying exactly the opposite of the last brilliant piece you read. The trick is no more than common sense. Weigh what you read by your past experience. Test the water before you dive in. If you strike gold, remember where. And also remember, that though the overuse of metaphors is indicative of poor writing, it is not necessarily indicative of bad advice.

chapter 11

developing a system

at the very least you'll remember what the hell you did

You have just spent some valuable hours of your precious time reading *Technical Trading Online*. The only cogent reason for doing so was to add to your knowledge of stock trading. If you do not apply this knowledge, then you have wasted your time. You cannot apply this knowledge if you forget it. The only way to keep from forgetting it, is to use it. The best way to use this newly acquired knowledge is often, and as part of a system. If you do not have a system, it is time to develop one.

Trading stocks through your own personal system offers a number of advantages. First of all, it allows you to do more things reflexively, which means faster. The ability to act reflexively frees your mind to focus on evaluations and options that do necessitate thought. The ability to act quickly, pure and simple, translates into greater profits, especially to the day trader. A refined system allows your mind to work decisively, in a straight ahead fashion instead of zigzagging all over the place. There is comfort in repetition, doing the same thing with the current stock that you have done with thousands of others. If unexpected problems arise, chances are you have handled similar ones before. If not, then the next time you will have. A tried and true system gives you the confidence to act decisively, and the clear head necessary to do so. It will help you keep your emotions in check, so as not to cloud decisions that should be made with cold calculation. It is when you stop and ask yourself, "What should I do now?" that fear takes hold. If you are already applying the next step in your system, you have no time to fear. According to Hollywood, "Greed is good." Well in this case, Hollywood is half right, admittedly quite an improvement. The only time greed is good is when it is in the other guy's eyes, not yours. A familiar system can keep greed in check. It is up to you to develop this system and also to cultivate the discipline to stick with it.

A system is not a magic formula that cannot fail. A system is a specific, disciplined, structured method of finding the right stock, watching it, deciding whether to take a position, determining when, immediately concocting an exit strategy, deciding not how much profit is possible, but rather how much will be prudent. Most important, the best system is worthless without the discipline to stick with it.

The time to develop your system is right now, when the techniques covered in this book are still fresh in your mind. Weigh their relevance and value, choosing the most insightful and dependable. I certainly hope your system begins with the Four Golden Rules of Stock Trading:

1. Cut your losses.
2. Let your profits run.
3. Trade with the trend.
4. Never average down your losing positions.

The other components are up to you. No matter how good the system you develop, it can be of little value if you do not apply it religiously. Applying it, you will learn the worth of each component. Do not hesitate to add and subtract techniques. Your system is not a proven theorem. It is an inexact tool that can be and should be refined.

chapter 12

the daily plan

if you want to make God laugh, tell Him your plans

As a sop to all you New Agers and Tony Robbins True Believers, it is jingle time again. Here goes: "If you don't have a plan, you are planning to fail." Ignore these words and someday they may enter your head and never leave. That's a thought that should scare you!

The following plan is in a day trader's timeframe, but easily expandable into that of any trader. However keep in mind that the day trader's trend is an inconsequential blip to the position trader, and the position trader's trend is about as relevant to the day trader as a light year is to a mayfly.

Your daily plan can be divided into three sections:

1. Pre-opening
2. Post-opening
3. Post-closing

A pre-opening strategy allows you to start trading at the opening bell.

pre-opening

- Check the daily and weekly charts to see if you can find stocks that can be located on our model.
- Apply stochastics and RSIs to these stocks, and look for buy or sell signals.

- Divide the stocks giving signals into stocks to be bought and stocks to be sold short, according to whichever trend takes hold.
- Decide whether they closed strong or weak, in anticipation of how they will open.
- Examine cash to futures ratio to predict where market is going.

post-opening

- Use the advance/decline index to determine the trend.
- Find the group or groups of stocks stronger than the uptrend or weaker than the downtrend.
- Within the stronger and weaker group or groups, find the stronger and weaker stocks.
- See if any of these stocks are in your pre-opening plan.
- Take a position based on buy or sell signals.
- Immediately, if not sooner, formulate an exit strategy.

post-close

- Analyze what you did and the results of what you did, finding and defining the relationships between cause and effect.
- Push your ego aside and if necessary modify your plans and methods.

Once you have an overall strategy and a daily plan, you must have the discipline to follow both, no matter how much your ego and emotions interfere. Let us say you buy long sure that a stock is going up, and low and behold, it drops below its mental stop. Even if that drop is only ⅛, you must have the discipline to sell. No matter if subsequent movement proves you wrong about the stock. You were not wrong to follow your plan. You can always modify your plan, but do so after the fact. In the heat of battle, trust your plan, not your ego or emotions.

chapter 13

cases

things you won't find in books, not usually

In this chapter, we make the anticipated, perhaps overly anticipated move from theory to practice. We are going to apply, step-by-step, many of the theories and techniques covered in this book. We shall follow some real stocks within the framework of real time. Unfortunately, you will notice that some of the real profits derived are far less than those accumulated in our previous fictitious examples. I am sure you realize that in those examples the exaggerations of price fluctuations and time were merely for clarity and to aid the learning process. There is no way I would have strayed from reality merely to keep your greedy little eyes wide open.

case 1

I'm the type that likes to start slow and finish fast, so we will begin these cases from the point of view of the position trader and his slightly more active cousin, the swing trader. Assume you are a position trader. A good night's sleep and a casual, comfortably late breakfast has left you in a satisfied mood. Hunting up a nice stock would increase your satisfaction. Casually, you head for your favorite hunting grounds, the interday charts. Today you just don't have the patience to get into stochastics and RSIs, so you decide to concentrate upon price and volume. A questionable decision where realism is concerned, but a fortunate, simplifying one for illustrative purposes.

The date is September 4, so your interday charts all end on September 3. The first one you come to, Figure 13.1, catches your eye. Morgan Stanley Dean Witter seems to be developing a trading range. The market is bullish, and you are willing to bet

figure 13.1   case 1, chart 1

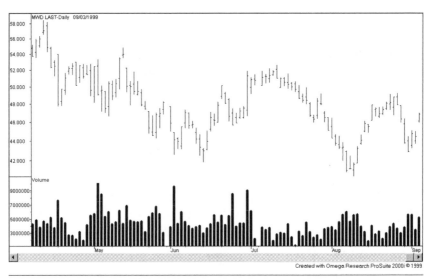

Source: Used with permission of Omega Research.

on a long term uptrend. If MWD is in an accumulation phase, this could very well lead to a markup phase and one of those long uptrends that are your bread and butter during rising markets. You will definitely have to come back to MWD, and that is exactly what you do, every single day. You even bring some of your swing trader friends along with you.

On September 29, the trading range has narrowed considerably, as we see in Figure 13.2. You are not sure what to make of this. Some of your swing trader friends have lost interest, but you haven't, not yet. On the October 15 chart, Figure 13.3, your interest is rewarded. You think you have yourself a fairly well defined trading range with a very generous spread. In fact, one of your swing trading buddies has profited nicely (Figure 13.4). On October 11, he goes short off resistance, then long on support on October 19. However, swing trading is

figure 13.2   case 1, chart 2

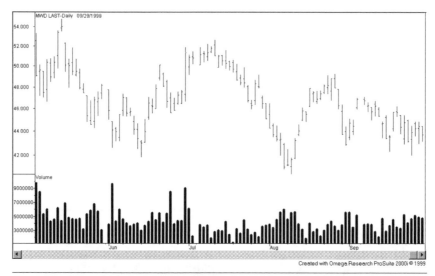

Source: Used with permission of Omega Research.

figure 13.3   case 1, chart 3

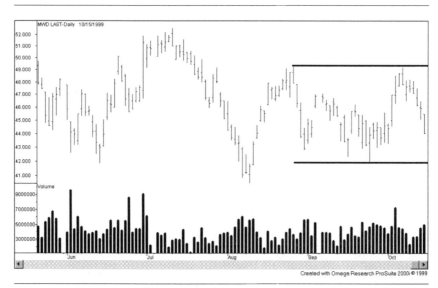

Source: Used with permission of Omega Research.

figure 13.4   case 1, chart 4

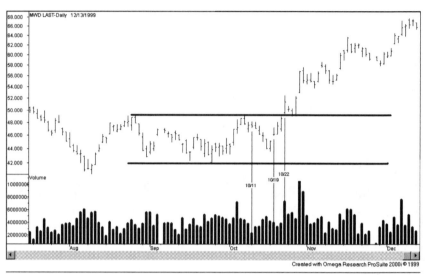

Source: Used with permission of Omega Research.

not your style. You are waiting for a break high and the long markup phase it may portend.

From Figure 13.4, we see that the break high came on October 22. Even more reassuring, it comes with strong volume. Some of your swing trader friends jump right on. The overnight traders had also shown interest, but were dissuaded by the fact that MWD did not close near its high for the day. The bread and butter of overnight traders are stocks that close at or very near their highs or lows, with enough momentum to keep them going into the next morning.

Battle hardened position traders like yourself are still not even tempted. You take your time, not like those slimy day traders ready to dive for a teeny ⅛ point profit. No, you want to see if there is a pullback after the break high, one with low volume that portends a fast recovery and a long markup phase. Sure enough, there is, and you are ready to make your move.

The third morning after the break high, MWD starts a steady rise. Day traders, rapacious eyes on their one- and five-minute charts, the scent of momentum in their nostrils, bare their fangs and pounce. You, of course, hold your ground and try to hide your disdain. This is made easier by your strong hunch that before the closing bell, you too will take a position in MWD. Yet you intend to do so in a civilized manner, and to hold that position for the long haul. Right now you want to see if this stock can keep its strength when the day traders waddle away with their stomachs full.

By late afternoon, the day traders have cashed out for the session, bragging about their profits, while stock price continues to rise. Overnight, swing, and position traders have provided enough demand to meet supply, and a touch more to boot. The overnight traders saw MWD's strength, looking as if it would close at or near its high for the day. They figured that this strength will carry over into the next day, with a good chance for a gap opening. A few minutes from the closing bell, MWD equals its break high. You're sold, taking a position, for 1000 shares and the long haul.

case 2

For the sake of convenience, and to save you the bother of flipping through figures, we will examine this next case in retrospect. For the sake of realism, we shall play close attention to the corresponding stochastic and RSI.

Let us assume that you are a swing trader. If you had happened upon Johnson & Johnson's (JNJ) chart (Figure 13.5) on August 2, 1999, and if you also happened to have read that fine book, *Technical Trading Online,* then you would have surely

figure 13.5   case 2, chart 1

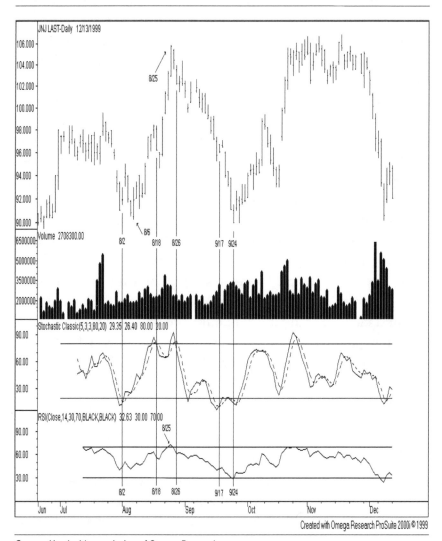

Source: Used with permission of Omega Research.

caught one very clear buy signal. On the stochastic, percentage K is crossing percentage D in the oversold area. You quickly check the RSI for confirmation. Unfortunately, the RSI is well above the buy zone. Also, volume has held fairly steady the last few days, adding nothing to your vast store of knowledge. You check the price chart looking for a trading range. You see something that could eventually turn into a trading range, especially if you stare at it long enough. That gets tiring, so you decide to just wait and see if these hen scratching will in fact turn into a trading range, one that will arrive with far stronger confirmation. This decision ends up costing you a very handsome profit. JNJ starts out on what will turn out to be a thirteen-point climb. You watch it shaking your head, mumbling, "That's life in the jungle." At least it did not cost you a cent of savings. Still, you have been staring at this stock a long time. It's about time you made some damn money off of it. Besides, since you were a kid you must have used a million of Johnson & Johnson's Band-Aids. Determined to get something out of this stock, you wait calmly for the chart gods to send you another sign.

You get just that on August 18. Percentage $K,$ the solid line of the stochastic crosses percentage D just inside the overbought zone. JNJ is about to close weak, at or very near its low. Seeing that it is also about to test its last high, you get a real itch to go short. Looking for confirmation, you see that though the RSI is heading south, it isn't near the sell zone. Experience tells you not to go short on the information you can derive from the chart. Yet a little voice in your head tells you to forget confirmation, that this stock is headed south, that it is time to get some money out of it. Now if you had the RSI even close to the buy zone, then you would tell that annoying little voice where to go. You don't. You won't. You side with the little voice over experience, selling 100 shares short. A quick glance at your money market account inspires the quick placement of a ½ point buy stop.

The next day, JNJ gaps open down and drops precipitously as the little voice whispers, "I told you so." Well this was the last time that day that you heard from the little voice. JNJ recovers and closes close to its opening price. The next day you are tempted to cover your short, but fight successfully against a fall into temptation. This matters little, because price rises enough to set off your ½ point automatic buy stop and closes you out. This shuts up the little voice, leaving you wondering, "Whose damn voice is that, anyway?" Over the next few days, you congratulate yourself on setting that automatic buy stop as you watch JNJ shoot up ten points.

Now this damn stock that is making everyone rich, actually owes you money. You are even more determined to make something off of it, which incidentally can be a very costly attitude, one well worth avoiding. In any case, you make up your mind to go by the chart the next chance you get. That chance comes a week later, on August 26. JNJ is about to close weak, at or near its low for the day. Just the day before, the RSI took a mouth watering fall out of the sell zone. Today the stochastic is giving you a sell signal. You take it, selling short.

A few days later the stochastic comes close to giving you an oversold signal. Still, it is not close enough to make you cover, especially without confirmation. On September 17, the stochastic gives you a strong, unequivocal oversold signal, but again the RSI fails to lend confirmation. In fact, it might be heading back up. You decide to hold tight, but with your finger on the eject button.

On September 24, you press that eject button on a very profitable trade. The RSI is in the buy zone and the stochastic looks poised to confirm. It does, the very next day. A nice rise in price comes along with it. So does the urge to go long. At the same time you decide to take out your pencil to draw a support line between the lows of August 6 and September 24 (Figure 13.6). It comes out nice and flat, so you go ahead and draw a parallel line through the high on August 25. This sure looks like a trading range to you. Now the stochastic and RSI really seem to be screaming at you to buy long. You do just that, going back to the well one more time. You even go right out to buy two packages of Band-Aids, fueling the upturn with some of your ready cash.

Now remember that pompous position trader from Case 1, just the type of snob that would turn his nose up at anything less than a markup or markdown phase. As a matter of fact, if I remember correctly, he happened to be you. Well he has been watching JNJ too. Don't be fooled by that nose in the air. As soon as no one is looking, the nose comes down and he is glad to sneak onto the swing trader's battlefield to take a strong yet surreptitious position in such a nice fat trading range.

Then it happens, possible trouble. On October 12, only halfway up to the resistance line you are expecting it to reach, JNJ pulls back a little. Also, you don't like the stochastic crossing so close to the sell zone. Still, it wasn't in it. If the RSI is giving a signal, it's in Greek. You decide to hold tight. Besides, your pompous position trading old self seems hardly to have noticed the dip.

On October 15, after three more days of decline, you are close to bailing out. Two things stop you. The stochastic looks as if it is heading for a crossing in the oversold zone. More important, a large drop in volume accompanies this decline, giving you confidence that it is only a short-lived reaction. In credit to your astute trading sense, that is exactly what it turns out to be.

figure 13.6   case 2, chart 2

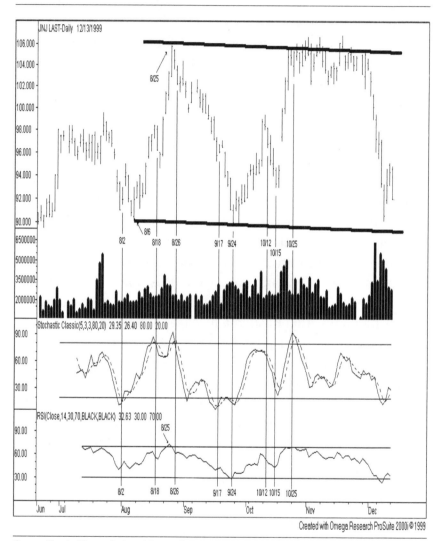

Source: Used with permission of Omega Research.

By October 25, stock price starts scraping along the resistance line. The stochastic yells, "Sell!" and the RSI whispers it. Well you the swing trader, and your high and mighty former self, the position trader, have both profited nicely. It is time to cash in and go to our next case.

case 3

Now you will see why we hurried through the last case. The next three cases are on day trading. Whatever prejudices you may have against day traders, you have to admit that these ferrets and otters are entertaining. Nobody holding a bottle of Ritalin ever caught up to one of these moving targets. As an added bonus, you will see that many day trading techniques apply equally well to position and swing trading. If you can keep up, you may learn something.

Now that I am taking you through a simplified day of trading, it is time to mention that the large majority of successful day traders divide their days into two sessions—9:30 A.M. to 11:30 A.M. and 1:30 P.M. to 4:00 P.M. They avoid 11:30 A.M. to 1:30 P.M. because of the drop in volume during this period, thus making a bad situation even worse by dropping volume even further, which in turn decreases liquidity and accents aberrations even more. For example, if a 10,000 share buy order hits the floor around noon, there probably won't be enough sellers to keep supply in balance with demand. The lack of volume alone will probably push up the stock's price even on a down day. This phenomenon is commonly referred to as the *noon balloon*. Successful traders seek certainty, not uncertainty.

The cases that follow involve typical trades. An accomplished trader may handle dozens of similar ones in a day. And he can handle hundreds just like them between those much talked about and seldom experienced killings. Since you took the first two cases, I'll take the next three. That does not mean you can relax. We are going to be moving fast. Hold on to your hats.

May 14, 1999 is an ordinary day for the stock market. We meet it with a game plan:

1. Examine the groups, looking for longs in the strong groups and shorts in the weak groups.
2. Determine the trend.
3. Take a position with the trend.
4. Decide on an exit strategy.
5. Take the loss or let the profits run, preferably the latter.

You snap on the television to CNBC. The first thing you want to know is whether the S&P Futures are up or down. As usual, the laws of the universe interfere. What you hear instead is that the Commerce Department has released the business inventory figures and the Labor Department has come out with the Consumer Price Index. The expected CPI numbers were +.04 percent/+.02 percent. The actual numbers came in at +.07 percent/+.04 percent. CNBC adds that these numbers point to a resumption of inflation. Now I could pad this book with at least five more boring pages explaining why. No doubt you are among that large majority of people who judge a book's value by it's weight. Well allow me to point out that not one bookstore in this wide, wide world has a butcher's scale alongside the cash register. Books are like airplanes—the lighter the better. So just follow my advice. When CNBC says that those figures way back at the beginning of this paragraph point to a resumption of inflation, take their word for it. Why would they lie? Besides, the day trader is more interested in the effect of the news than the news itself. Of course there should be a predictable cause-and-effect relationship between the two. Just don't bet on said predictability.

It so happens that on May 14, a lot of professional futures traders did take CNBC's word for it and acted accordingly. These boys do not like inflation, not at all. Their previous optimism was replaced by pessimism. They not only sold the S&P 500 Futures that they were long, they shorted additional ones. These pros know what they are doing, so you would be advised not to spend too much time wondering why. Do so, and you may miss a very profitable ride.

H.L. Camp and CNBC come out with Fair Value, pegging it at 4.76 over. Translated, this means that if the S&P Futures contract is valued at 4.76 over cash, then the cash to futures relationship is where it should logically be. An imperfect relationship with an illogical gap large enough to contain a locked in profit would of course arouse the arbitragers. Their activity should narrow the gap in the direction of Fair Value. If said activity fails to do so, and the gap widens, the computer generated programs will come riding on in like the cavalry. Believe me, you want to be riding with them, not standing in front of them.

Our TV talking heads tell us that the computer buy programs will kick in if futures over cash hits 7.24. Now this figure is the reason they invented pens, pencils, and computer keyboards. Write it down and keep it in front of you. If the cost of futures goes to 7.24 over when Fair Value is 4.76, then the price of the stocks involved makes them look like a bargain by comparison, even to the computers. If they do not crash from the excitement, the computer programmed traders will immediately commence buying the stocks and selling the futures. This is no time for the day trader to be taking a nap.

Our TV talking heads also tell us that sell programs will enter at 2.48 futures over cash. Allow me to avoid specifics here and merely state that this will trigger the exact same response as futures over cash hitting 7.24, only bass ackwards. Do not worry if you don't completely understand this process. Believe me, after you have lost a few hundred thousand dollars, it will begin to sink in.

Back to the boards. Well S&P Cash had closed the day before at 1367^{56}, while S&P Futures closed at 1375. Today S&P Futures opened at 1350, a gap down of 25 points. Against yesterdays close of S&P Cash, futures are worth less. Something has to give and it is S&P Cash. When the market opens at 9:30 A.M., the S&P 500 Index drops to 1347^{61}. Here it is May 14, summer coming on strong, and despite this the market is heading south.

Well Rule 3 is, "Trade with the trend." Obviously, the trend is down, but that does not stop us from looking for confirmation. At 9:48 A.M., we've got 414 advancing issues/1943 declining. No ambiguity about those figures. I'm raring to take some short positions, but good breeding and discipline force me to check some indexes. At 9:50 A.M.:

Dow Jones Industrials	10997^{94}	-110^{54}
Dow Jones Transports	3696^{77}	-55^{19}
Dow Jones Utilities	316^{94}	-3^{45}
Composite Index	3323^{28}	-43^{01}
S&P 500	1346^{57}	-20^{85}

If that was not confirmation, nothing is. It is time to check out the groups:

Consumers	Down
Semiconductors	Down

Heavy Construction	Mixed
Entertainment	Down
Airlines	Down
Autos	Down
Toys	Down
Software	Down
Healthcare	Down
Restaurants	Mixed
Footwear	Down
Advertising	Down
Financials	Down
Oil Drillers	Up
Gold	Up
Real Estate Trusts	Mixed
Computers	Down

We have quite a choice of down groups in which to search for stocks to short. Let's try airlines. Within this group, American Airlines (AMR) looks very weak (see Figure 13.7). It closed at 74, and gapped open down 1½ at 72½. At 9:42 A.M. it makes a low of 71¹⁵⁄₁₆.

I refuse to get into a drawn out psychological explanation here, so just take my word for it that those traders who bought American Airlines long at the opening bell expected it to go up not down. Well it didn't. Now, most of these traders will be happy to get even by bailing out 72½ or close to it. This makes 72½ a line of resistance. To short, we have to wait for an uptick, and we want to do so on a bounce anyway. However, if AMR breaks that line of resistance by beating its opening price, all bets are off.

At 9:52 A.M., we get the bounce we are waiting for in AMR and the market as a whole. AMR goes up to 72⅜, just below

figure 13.7   case 3

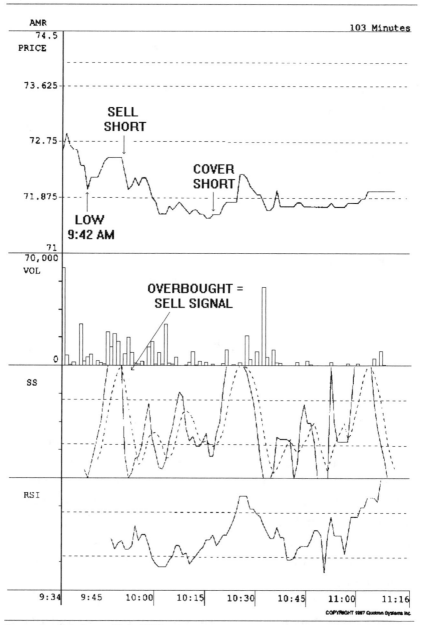

Source: Copyright Reuters Limited 2000.

resistance. On top of that, its stochastic is giving a sell signal. And the S&P Futures are getting weak again. This points to another wave of selling.

If we are going to get off the fence at all, the time is now. We sell AMR short at 72⅜, with a ⅜ buy stop above the entry. This places the stop at 72¾, ¼ above that 72½ opening price resistance line. Now it's time to wait and watch. (See Figure 13.7 for graphs of share price, volume, stochastic, and RSI.)

9:54 A.M.	AMR drops to 71¹⁵⁄₁₆, then starts a slow, gradual rise that does not come close to the stop at 72¾.
10:02 A.M.	Share price has dropped further to 71½. Looking good. Wait and watch.
10:20 A.M.	Indicator checks reveal:

Advances 475/Declines 2108

S&P 500 Cash 1341⁶⁰

S&P 500 Futures 1346⁵⁰

Futures Over Cash 4.90

Buy programs will trigger at 7.24. This bears careful watching, especially as to direction of movement. Better start thinking about risks vs. rewards, and conditions for bailing out.

RSI is on the rise, coming out of an oversold position and indicating a likely bounce.

10:22 A.M.	AMR is starting to move up. Its stochastic is heading north. Time to take your profits. Close out position by covering short at 71⅞.

Your profit is ½ point times 1000 shares, which equals $500 less commissions. Admittedly, this is not quite enough to retire on. Still, you have paid for this book, with enough left over for a second-hand laptop computer. Sure, you anticipated a lot more, more than the market wanted to give you. Never, never try to take more than the market wants to give you. The market, not your needs or wants, determines when you should take your profits. This has been a typical trade. Its results are nothing to be ashamed of. In fact, you have more capital now to cover your losses and keep you in the game until one of those few and far between killings comes along. While you are waiting, remember that the stock does not respond to the trader. The trader responds to the stock.

case 4

On May 18, 1999, following two down days, the market opens:

Dow Jones Industrials	10849[79]
Previous Day's Close	10853[47]
S&P 500	1339[49]
Previous Day's Close	1339[49]

9:38 A.M.

S&P Cash	1339[26]
S&P Futures	1343[50]
Fair Value Futures Over Cash	4.33
Buy Programs	6.72
Sell Programs	2.04

9:40 A.M.

984 Advancing issues/887 Declining issues
This slightly bullish bias should pry your eyes open a tad.

Trader's Index (TRIN)   0.91
> This indicator is also slightly bullish. There could be a rally in the making.

Better find a strong stock in a strong group. We may be going long very soon.

Telephones	Strong
Computers	Strong

Tel Mexico (TMX) looks interesting. (See Figure 13.8.)

9:44 A.M.

> TMX makes high, pulls back, breaks high.
>
> Buy TMX at 84⅝ with a ⅜ sell stop at 84¼. (Note that stop is below last trough.)
>
> Watch and wait.

9:54 A.M.

> 1219 Advancing issues/903 Declining issues
>
> Traders Index (TRIN)   0.79
>
> Both indicators are getting stronger. So is your blood's adrenaline content.

10:10 A.M. (See Figure 13.9.)

> TMX makes high, pulls back, then tests high. The high passes the test and TMX fails it.
>
> Yet the Dow Industrials and the S&P 500 are still going higher.
>
> Yet stochastic and RSI are both screaming overbought and to sell?
>
> Go with the failed test of the high and the stochastic and RSI. Sell at 85⅛ for ½ point profit.

---

figure 13.8   case 4, chart 1

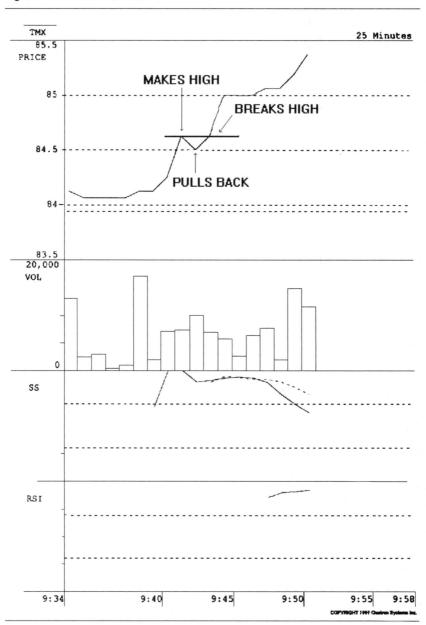

Source: Copyright Reuters Limited 2000.

figure 13.9   case 4, chart 2

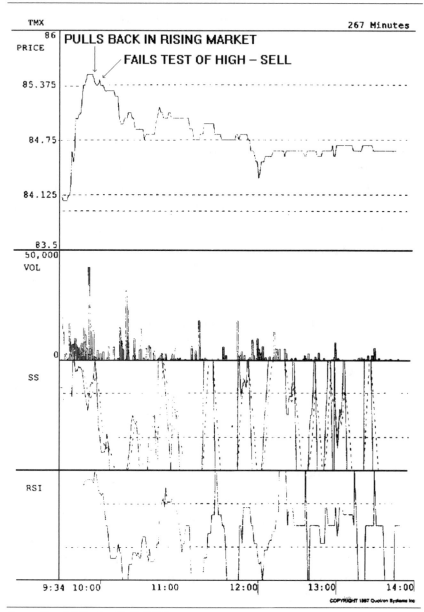

Source: Copyright Reuters Limited 2000.

TMX looks like a good short, but both the Dow and S&P 500 are still up. The advance/decline is still positive. You might make some money by breaking Rule 3 and trading against the trend, but you'll flunk this day trader's course.

case 5

On May 18, 1999, the same day as Case 4, but a few hours later, Alan Greenspan, head of the Federal Reserve Bank, speaks for a few hours. As usual, no one can figure out what the hell he says. Also as usual, yours truly is the only person willing to admit his ignorance. The market gives signs of reversing downward.

2:15 P.M.

Advancing issues 1388/Declining issues 1491.

The trend has reversed.

Find a short, quick.

Oops! I did say quick. Sell programs hit, and yours truly misses the ride down. Maybe there will be a bounce I can catch.

2:26 P.M. (See Figure 13.10.)

Merrill Lynch (MER) breaks low, rallies back, and then turns down again. Too bad I missed the 2:05 P.M. sell short signal, a failed test of a high. Missing the next one, the break in support, is even more embarrassing. No time to worry about that now. Short at 79⅞ with a ⅜ stop at 80¼.

figure 13.10   case 5

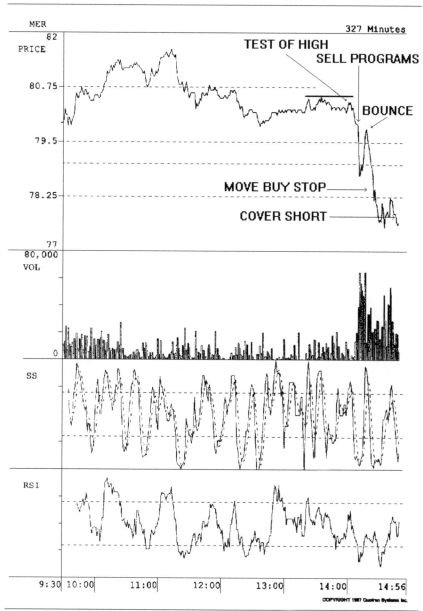

Source: Copyright Reuters Limited 2000.

2:32 P.M.

> MER is falling, a little bounce, then resumes downward.
>
> Protect profits by lowering stop down to 78⅜.

2:49 P.M.

> MER makes a low and tests it, giving signs of bottoming.
>
> Think about covering short. 77⅝ looks like a good place to do it.
>
> In the meantime, just watch and wait.

2:53 P.M.

> MER is developing a base.
>
> Time to cover short at 77¾.
>
> 1⅛ point times 1000 shares gives a profit of $1125.

The five cases we covered were typical trades. Of course all trades do not end profitably. Those that don't do limited damage if your stops are in the right places. If you want an example of a losing trade, just imagine one of the previous cases being stopped out. Then again, make a few trades and you will have no need to imagine.

chapter 14

breaking the rules

live fast, die young, and have a good-looking corpse (in the pauper's graveyard)

Chapter 2 contained the Four Golden Rules of Stock Trading. I stand by them. Still, it is important that you become familiar with trading techniques that break these rules, if for no other reason than to be able to spot their effects upon the market. Realistically, I know some of you will, despite my advice, try these techniques. I would equate this to running a red light at three in the morning. The streets are deserted. No one is in sight. Without any cross traffic, you don't have to worry about an accident. There seems no chance that a cop lies in wait. However, there is only one way to be sure—run the light. Yet is your gain of a minute or two really worth the chance? If you decide it is, don't go looking for sympathy if you get caught. Whatever odds you bucked, they would have been better if you had obeyed the rules. The same is true for the Four Golden Rules of Stock Trading.

No one day trades stocks very long before hearing the terms "fade the opening" or "short the gap." This refers to a popular technique that involves trading against the trend in a rising market. Let us say that pre-opening, cash to futures is a quite bullish 20 over. You can bet that more than one stock will open with an imbalance of demand over supply. To attract the necessary supply, they will gap open. This means opening prices will be higher than the previous day's closing prices.

In Figure 14.1, at Point 2, we see that our particular stock opened at $84. This is $4 dollars higher than the previous day's close at Point 1. This price jump will entice some profit takers to sell and increase supply. Some other traders are sure to jump on this gap and sell short at $84. This is called *fading the opening* or *shorting the gap*, which also increases supply. This

figure 14.1 fading the opening

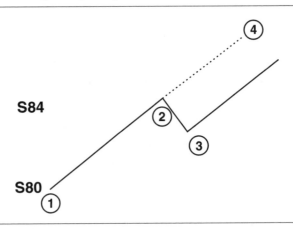

increased supply should drive down the share price, to Point 3 in Figure 14.1. Clearly, these traders are breaking Rule 3, Trade with the Trend. Like our friend who runs the red light, they may very well get away with it. Then again, they may not. For a myriad of possible reasons, share price may instead rise along the dotted line to Point 4.

However, let us say that share price does drop as planned to $83 at Point 3. You personally would never think of trading against the trend. The market is bullish and you are buying long or playing the wallflower. What have you learned from the example illustrated in Figure 14.1? One thing you should have learned, unless you are into roller coasters, is not to get caught up in the hoopla and jump in to buy at the opening bell. What is the point of riding this stock down from Point 2 to Point 3? The place to jump on is right after confirmation, just past Point 3. Not only do you save a point on the purchase price, your entire ride is up. And you probably won't have to wait long. The reversal after Point 3 often occurs within 20 minutes of the opening bell.

breaking the rules

Another possibility, and a nice one, is that you had bought the stock the previous day for some now obviously brilliant reason, and you kept an overnight position. Even if you are confident of a further rise in share price after a small fade, you could still make a case to sell near Point 2, then buy back again just after Point 3. However, you better keep your eyes glued to your monitor and your fingers resting on your keyboard.

chapter 15

conclusion

the first million dollars is always the hardest

Amidst the hoopla surrounding today's stock market, the very hype that probably caused you to pick up this book, forgive me for stating a tragic little fact. Even in this rising market, a significant number of traders have lost a significant amount of money. Furthermore, I would bet my entire stash of thirty-year treasury bonds that the large majority of would-be day traders ended up in this unhappy group. Unless you too aspire to join up, you better ask yourself why so many people fail. If you don't know the answer, you haven't been paying attention—lack of knowledge and lack of discipline.

Don't ever forget that knowledge is more valuable than profit, especially to the inexperienced, and most especially to the day trader. Learn from every trade. What you lose in money, gain in skill. It is not enough to critique each trade individually. You must also examine each trading day as a whole. At first worry only about the trades you have made. Later, much later, you can start critiquing trades you should have made. If you can derive a general, cogent, applicable reason for making such trades in the future, then give it a try. If not, then don't let missed profits affect your subsequent decisions.

It will not take you long to realize that your most important lessons will come from losing trades. Protect your capital by keeping these losses as small as possible. You must also protect some of your profits, squirreling them away for the dry spells. The novice should operate with a single principle foremost: preserve your capital so as to stay in the game until you can master it. Increase the stakes very, very gradually. I mean over years, not over months. Traders, particularly day traders, that go in for the kill, are themselves likeliest to get killed.

I have done my best to minimize the use of technical terms in this book, but in conclusion I must mention a few that cannot, or at least should not, be avoided. There is an often heard term for the novice that would read a book such as *Technical Trading Online,* then immediately start day trading stocks. In the business, such a person is technically referred to by the term "idiot." If said person does this trading with money he or she cannot afford to just throw away, then the applicable technical term is "complete idiot."

Perhaps, up to this point, you are not quite sure the price you paid for *Technical Trading Online* was worth the knowledge gained. Well, allow me to take one last stab at winning you over. I will give you a tip that, if you have not thought of it yourself, is worth many times the cost of this book. As long as you follow it faithfully, I will not only guarantee that you will not lose one red cent, I also guarantee that you will not embarrass yourself. Now here is the tip: Do not use real money. Polish your techniques and learn from your mistakes. Only after the Monopoly money starts piling up, and with no guarantee from me, find an online brokerage firm and try risking a little real moolah. At first have the discipline to limit yourself to a few choice trades of small lots, one hundred shares maximum. Avoid thin stocks in favor of the higher volume more liquid issues.

Attitude, in stock trading as in almost every other endeavor, is crucial to success. However, different endeavors necessitate different attitudes. Trading stocks, you are competing against other traders, pitting your knowledge, skill, and speed against theirs. There are lessons to be learned every day. You better learn them, because at least some of your competition is doing just that. A prize fighter that stops training before he retires gets retired by someone else. The day you stop training is the day you stop improving. It should also be the day you stop trading stocks. You must face every day determined to build upon your knowledge, your skill, and your discipline as a stock trader in the same way each succeeding floor of a skyscraper is built upon the floor below. Understand that training is an ongoing progression, not a finite event.

Trading stocks is hard, serious work. You must be willing to do this work. *Technical Trading Online* gave you more than knowledge. It gave you techniques. Apply them. Customize them. Perfect them. Make these techniques your own. This book can do no more than point you in the right direction, tell you some of the things to look for and lookout for. *Technical Trading Online* will enable you to face the stock market at eye level. The market itself will be your final teacher and the refiner of your skills.

There is no point in my wishing you good luck, certainly no practical point. Forget about luck. It evens out. The less you think about it, the less you will depend upon or even hope for it. When pondering a trading decision, never take luck, good or bad, into consideration. That is a sure formula for losing. The stock trader should not be any more concerned about luck than the ditch digger. Just follow the rules and guidelines you set for yourself, fine tuning them through experience. Take things slow, but the sooner you start the better. In fact, the time to start is now.

glossary

abandon a position   Sell a stock that you own or buy (cover) a stock that you had sold short.

accumulation   See **accumulation trading range.**

accumulation phase   See **accumulation trading range.**

accumulation trading range   A trading range in which a particular stock is removed from the market by its purchasers in anticipation of an uptrend (see Figure 2.3).

ACPS   The average cents per share (up or down) of all stocks listed on the New York Stock Exchange.

advance/decline index   The preeminent indicator of market movement, calculated as the ratio of Advancing Issues over Declining Issues.

advancing issues   Stocks above their previous close.

arms index   See **trader's index.**

ascending triangle   A trend reversal signal, indicating the reversal of a downtrend (see Figure 4.7).

automatic stop loss order   A sell order that is only executed if a stock drops to a price specified by the seller, whereupon it becomes a market order.

balance sheet   An accounting statement listing assets and liabilities.

bear   Someone who believes the market will start to or continue to decline.

bearish   See **bear.**

break high   A break in resistance.

break low   A break in support.

break in resistance   An increase in stock price significantly higher than the stock's resistance line.

break in support   A drop in stock price significantly below that stock's support line.

brokerage customer's free balances   Cash available within brokerage accounts for the purchase of stock.

bull   Someone who believes the market will start to or continue to rise.

bullish   See **bull.**

buy long   Simply purchase a stock.

buy stop order   A buy order which is only executed if a stock reaches a specified price. It becomes a market order if and when stock price trades at that specified price.

call   The option to buy a specified number of shares at a specified price within a specified period of time.

candlesticks   A superior charting technique developed in Japan. It displays data in a manner that facilitates quick, thorough, and easy analysis.

certificate of deposit   A certificate representing a cash sum deposited for a fixed length of time at a fixed rate of interest.

comparative relative strength A stock's relative strength or weakness when compared to a market index such as the S&P 500 or the Dow Jones Industrial Average.

confirmation Agreement among indicators as to future price movement, as opposed to divergence, which is disagreement.

consolidation A pause in upward price movement that will end in continuation of that upward movement.

consumer price index Sometimes referred to as the cost-of-living index, it is an index that compares the price of basic goods and services to a fixed base period.

continuation signal An indication that a trend will continue, such as the appearance of the Isosceles Triangle or Flag pattern on a graph.

contra-trend trading See **trading against the trend.**

cover a short The abandoning of a short position by buying the stock you had originally sold short. See **sell short.**

CPI See **consumer price index.**

crossover The switching of a stock (or average, etc.) from an advancing to declining issue or vice versa. This is often highlighted by the switching of an indicator light or the stock's price from red to green or vice versa.

day+ext. hours Regular trading hours on one specified day, plus the extended hours both before and after that day when available. This is an option or condition specified in a stock order.

day trader A stock trader who buys a stock with the usual intention of selling it in a few minutes or a few hours, and absolutely no intention of keeping it overnight. He or she can easily take and abandon fifty stock positions in a day, some of them lasting only seconds.

declining issues   Stocks below their previous close.

descending triangle   A trend reversal signal, indicating the reversal of a uptrend (see Figure 4.7).

distribution   See **distribution trading range.**

distribution phase   See **distribution trading range.**

distribution trading range   A trading range in which an accumulated stock is sold off, distributed back into the market, because those holding it believe its upward price movement has come to an end (see Figure 2.3).

divergence   Disagreement among indicators as to future price movement, as opposed to confirmation, which is agreement.

DJIA   See **Dow Jones industrial average.**

doji   An almost bodiless candlestick representing no change or a very slight change in stock price (see Figure 3.6, Stock H).

doji evening star   This candlestick appears during an uptrend, representing a gap opening up and a subsequent closing at or very near this opening price. It is one of the strongest reversal patterns (see Figure 3.9).

doji morning star   This candlestick appears during a downtrend, representing a gap opening down and a subsequent closing at or very near the same price. It is one of the strongest reversal patterns (see Figure 3.9).

double bottom   A reversal signal, indicating the possibility of an imminent upturn. It consists of two very similar troughs in a graph (see Figure 4.5).

double top   A reversal signal, indicating the possibility of an imminent downturn. It consists of two very similar peaks on a graph (see Figure 4.5).

Dow Jones Industrial Average   A price-weighted average of thirty industrial stocks. It is the grand daddy of all averages, respected more for its age than its usefulness.

downtrend   A decrease in value over a relative length of time.

Dow theory   A trend indicator based upon confirmation or divergences of the Dow Jones Industrials, Transports, and Utilities Indexes.

ECN   See **electronic communications network.**

EDAT   See **electronic direct access trading.**

electronic communications network   A network such as Island that enables customer traders to meet among themselves and provides them all with the same information, such as its full book of bids and offers to better gauge a market.

electronic direct access trading   EDAT gives the trader direct access to the market. The connection is usually by a dedicated phone line. Using a mouse and keyboard, the trader buys the stock himself almost instantaneously, and without a broker as intermediary. Downloads are lightning fast.

engulfing pattern   A candlestick pattern that signals a possible reversal of trend. It occurs when the newest candlestick represents both a lower opening and a higher close than the previous candlestick. This larger bodied candlestick can be either black or white, but it must be the opposite color of the previous candlestick which it engulfs (see Figure 3.8).

enter a position   To buy a stock, or sell a stock short.

entrance strategy A checklist of self-selected conditions that, if met, recommend the taking of a position.

exit strategy A checklist of self-selected conditions that, if met, recommend the abandoning of a position.

extended hours Those hours before a market's opening and after its close when trading can take place outside of that market.

fair value A statistic that takes into account the fact that $100 in your possession today is worth more than a guaranteed $100 three months from now.

flag A continuation signal, found on a graph, resembling a flag. Low volume lends confirmation to this pattern.

flow of funds indicators Indicators such as Mutual Funds Cash, Hedge Funds Cash, Insurance Company Cash, Bank Customer's Cash, and Brokerage Customer's Free Balances. They gauge not only the flow of cash, but also its availability.

futures contract An agreement to deliver a commodity or a financial settlement at a specified date in the future.

gap open When a stock's opening price is significantly higher than the previous day's high or lower than the previous day's low.

gold futures An agreement to deliver gold or a financial settlement at a specified date in the future.

group indexes Indexes of particular industries such as oil, airline, pharmaceuticals, and so on.

GTC Good Till Cancelled—a term added to a stock order to keep it open and ready to be executed until triggered by market conditions. Depending upon the broker, it can really mean only a limited period such as thirty days.

GTC+ext. hours Good Till Cancelled—a term added to a stock order to keep it open and ready to be executed, during both regular and extended hours, until triggered by market conditions. Depending upon the broker, it can really mean only a limited period such as thirty days.

hammer A bullish candlestick during a downtrend that indicates a possible reversal of that trend. The same shape as a hanging man, if white it tells us that a serious price drop ended in a recovery, and that the stock closed up. A black hammer is only slightly less bullish (see Figure 3.7).

hanging man A candlestick with a very small or no upper wick. The defining feature is that the lower wick must be at least twice as long as the body. It can be black or white, but it has to occur during an uptrend. If you can picture the very small upper wick as a head, and the long lower wick as legs, then you can actually picture this candlestick as a hanging man. This candlestick indicates a possible loss of upward momentum and a reversal of trend (see Figure 3.7).

head and shoulders The most famous reversal signal—a pointed head flanked by pointed shoulders. High volume lends confirmation to this signal (see Figure 4.4).

hedge fund An investment fund that uses high-risk techniques in quest of large capital gains.

index An indicator such as the Standard & Poor's 500.

indicator An index, average, graph pattern, and so on, used to predict future behavior.

inflation A rise in the cost of goods or services.

inside quote The highest current bid and lowest offer on a stock.

insolvency   Bankruptcy.

institutional investor   Mutual funds, hedge funds, insurance companies, banks, Warren Buffett, and so on.

isosceles triangle   A continuation of trend signal that appears on graphs when a trading range narrows symmetrically and the triangle formed is neither ascending nor descending. With this signal, you will usually see a decrease in volume accompany the decrease in range. Then when the trend resumes there should be a jump in volume. However, if the trading range continues beyond the triangle tip, this is an indication that our signal is no signal at all. Anything can happen, and all bets are off (see Figure 4.8).

kinematic   Concerning motion itself, without regard to forces creating this motion.

level II screen   A screen, provided by an information service, which displays all bids and offers.

limited liability corporation   A form of business favored by day trading firms. The trader contributes his share of the corporation's capital, let's say $50,000, and theoretically he is a partner. The funds of all traders are comingled, thus allowing leverage of 10 to 1 or more, instead of the standard 2 to 1, commonly referred to as regulation T margins.

limit order   A stock order that includes a limit price. If the market price is lower than the limit price, the buyer receives the stock at the lower market price. If the market price is higher, no buy is executed and he is protected from spending more than he cares to. Of course, in this case, he has failed to buy the stock.

LLC   See **limited liability corporation.**

MACD oscillator Moving average convergence-divergence oscillator, known for the infallibility of its hindsight.

major market index (XMI) An option index which closely mirrors the movement of the Dow Jones Industrial Average.

markdown phase The period of downward price movement that often follows a distribution trading range.

market order A stock order that will be executed at the market price when the order is received. This is the only way to be sure you get a stock, but you cannot be sure how much you will have to pay. Usually, the price will be close to the quick quote, but a sudden run on the stock is a dangerous possibility.

market structure indicator Indicators concerned with, among other things, price trends, cycles, volume, and their inter-relationships. Examples of market structure indicators are the Standard & Poor's Cash to Futures Relationship, the Trader's Index, the ACPS, and so on.

markup phase The period of upward price movement that often follows an accumulation trading range.

mutual fund An investment fund that manages the capital of its investors.

odd lot sales Sales of less than 100 shares at a time.

OBV See **on balance volume.**

OEX See **S&P 100 index.**

on balance volume (OBV) A calculation used to detect if a stock is under accumulation or distribution.

online Connected to the internet.

online trader A trader connected to a broker through the internet. The broker acts as an intermediary between trader and stock market. Download times can be long and costly. See **electronic direct access trading** for comparison.

order screen   The Web page of an online broker or the screen provided by an information service that allows you to buy and sell stock with mouse or keyboard.

oscillator   A graphical indicator used to predict when a market is overbought or oversold, and therefore in line for a reversal of trend.

overbought   The condition of a market when the buyers, who have overreacted, are about to turn into or give way to the sellers, thus precipitating a drop in price.

overbought area   See **overbought zone.**

overbought signal   A sell signal, such as given by a stochastic when Percentage K, the solid line, crosses Percentage D, the dotted line in the upper area of the graph designated as the overbought zone.

overbought zone   The upper area, often 20 percent, of an oscillator's graph. It is separated from the lower 80% by a horizontal line.

overnight traders   Traders who usually wait until between 3:00 and 4:00 P.M. to put on positions. If they think a stock is going to continue in an uptrend the next morning, or perhaps even gap open, they buy long. If they think it is going to continue in a downtrend, they sell short. Ideally, they have closed out all their positions by 11:00 A.M. the next morning.

oversold   The condition of a market when the sellers, who have overreacted, are about to turn into or give way to the buyers, thus precipitating a rise in price.

oversold area   See **oversold zone.**

oversold signal   A buy signal, such as given by a stochastic when Percentage K, the solid line, crosses Percentage D, the dotted line in the bottom area of the graph designated as the oversold zone.

oversold zone   The lower area, often 20 percent, of an oscillator's graph. It is separated from the upper 80 percent by a horizontal line.

pennant   A continuation signal, found on a graph, resembling a pennant. Low volume tends to confirm this pattern.

pent up demand   The desire to buy that has for some reason been held in check.

percentage D   The dotted line of the stochastic, it is a moving average of the Percentage K line, and therefore the slower moving of the two.

percentage K   The faster, solid line of a stochastic, it is the result of a complicated mathematical formula that takes into consideration momentum, rate of change, and range comparisons.

point of supply   Where supply enters a market driving down price.

position trader   A trader who buys stocks with the intention of keeping them for at least a few weeks.

price/earnings ratio   The price of a share of stock divided by the per share dollar amount of the company's earnings.

price markdown   A decrease in price.

price markdown phase   Sustained price movement in a generally downward direction.

price markup   An increase in price.

price markup phase   Sustained price movement in a generally upward direction.

price spread   Usually referring to a stock caught in a trading range, the price spread is the difference between the upper and lower limits of this range. This is opposed to "the spread," usually the difference between the bid and asked prices of a stock.

profit taking   Abandoning a profitable position.

put   The option to sell a specified number of shares at a specified price within a specified period of time.

put/call ratio   A sentiment indicator. When there is a high ratio of puts to calls, mass sentiment is predicting that the market is heading down. However, the successful stock trader is aware of the truth in that hallowed proverb, "The masses are asses."

quick quote   A complete stock quote—high, low, last sale, change, volume, yield, and so on.

quote screen   A computer monitor screen that displays one or more stock quotes. They range from the Spartan ones offered by some Web sites to the intricately informative and easy to use screens provided by the better information services.

real-time quotes   Up to the second quotes, as opposed to delayed quotes.

relative strength   See **comparative relative strength.**

relative strength index   See **RSI.**

resistance line   A line on a graph, often drawn by connecting two peaks, which represents a supposed limit that price movement is having trouble crossing.

reversal of trend   The changing of an uptrend into a downtrend, or vice versa.

RSI   An oscillator derived from a complicated formula that takes into consideration not only a stocks selling price, but also trading volume and other factors. Though a relative strength index, it is very different from the relative strength, in that the RSI measures a stock's relative strength compared to itself as opposed to an index.

S&P cash market   See **Standard & Poor's cash market.**

S&P cash to futures   See **Standard & Poor's cash to futures index.**

S&P 500   See **Standard & Poor's 500 index.**

S&P futures market   See **Standard & Poor's futures market.**

S&P 100 index (OEX)   See **Standard & Poor's 100 index.**

S&P wave   See **Standard & Poor's wave.**

selling short   Selling a stock you do not own by borrowing it from your broker. This is done in the belief that the stock price will fall and with the intention of eventually buying it (covering your short) at a lower price. Your profit or loss will be calculated by subtracting transaction fees and the price you will pay for the stock from the current price, minus interest paid to the broker for borrowing the stock.

sell short stop order   A sell short order for entry purposes, that lies dormant until a stock rises or falls to a specified price, whereupon the order becomes a market order to sell short.

sentiment indicators   Indicators that deal with psychology. They monitor groups of people—some usually right about the market and some usually wrong—and draw conclusions based upon the behavior of these groups. For example, the Put/Call Ratio is one of these sentiment indicators. When there is a high ratio of puts to calls, mass sentiment is predicting that the market is heading down. However, mass sentiment is usually wrong. Therefore, a high Put/Call Ratio is actually indicating an imminent rise in the market.

short covering   The abandoning of a short position by buying the stock you had originally sold short. See **sell short.**

spread   Usually refers to the difference between the bid and asked prices of a stock. This is opposed to a "price spread," which usually concerns a stock caught in a trading range, and is the difference between the upper and lower price extremes of this range.

Standard & Poor's cash market   The actual current cash value of the stocks in the Standard & Poor's 500 Index.

Standard & Poor's cash to futures index   The relationship of the Standard & Poor's Cash Market to the nearest Standard & Poor's Futures Contract.

Standard & Poor's 500 index   A weighted index of stock prices for 500 large companies. This index is a respected indicator of stock market trends.

Standard & Poor's futures market   The value of a particular S&P 500 contract at any moment in time.

Standard & Poor's 100 index (OEX)   An options index of 100 Standard & Poor's stocks, that closely mirrors the Standard & Poor's 500 Index.

Standard & Poor's wave   Slang for an intraday movement in the Standard & Poor's Futures Contract.

glossary

stochastic   A dynamic indicator, consisting of a fast line and a slow line, that gives buy and sell signals according to crossovers in overbought and oversold zones.

stop limit order   This type of order is most often used if a cautious trader suspects a stock is about to break resistance and go into a markup phase. The placed order lies dormant unless the stock hits a specified price, whereupon it will be filled at that price or not at all.

stop loss order   When holding a long position, a sell order that turns into a market order when a stock trades through a specified price. When holding a short position, a buy order that turns into a market order when the stock trades through a specified price.

stop order   A buy or sell order at a specific price that becomes a market order when and if the stock trades through that price. A stop order can be used as an entry strategy.

support line   A line on a graph, often drawn by connecting two troughs, which represents a supposed lower limit that price movement is having trouble crossing.

swing trader   A trader who usually keeps positions from a few days to a few weeks.

take a position   To buy a stock or sell a stock short.

trader's index:

$$\frac{\text{Advancing issues} / \text{Declining issues}}{\text{Advancing volume} / \text{Declining volume}} = N$$

If N is >1, the market is bearish. If N is <1, the market is bullish. The value of N is of interest, but of greater interest are changes in N.

trading range   A phase in price movement (stock, index, etc.) in which price fluctuations take on a redundant pattern, price more or less oscillating between two values.

trading against the trend   Buying long in a downtrend and selling short in an uptrend, sometimes referred to as contra-trend trading.

trading with the trend   Buying long in an uptrend and selling short in a downtrend.

trend   Price movement in one general direction, either up or down.

triple bottom   A reversal signal, indicating the possibility of an imminent upturn, consisting of three very similar troughs in a graph. It could also be called a trading range (see Figure 4.6).

triple top   A reversal signal, indicating the possibility of an imminent downturn, consisting of three very similar peaks in a graph. It could also be called a trading range (see Figure 4.6).

uptrend   An increase in value over a relative length of time.

XMI   See **major market index.**

zero line   The horizontal median line of an oscillator.

index